PORTFOLIO

HOW TO THRIVE IN
A FAMILY BUSINESS

Ajay Sharma is the director and promoter of Shree Baidyanath
Ayurved Bhawan Pvt. Ltd—the largest manufacturer of Ayurvedic
medicines in India. One of the strong pillars in the third generation
of the first family of Ayurveda—Baidyanath—he has been a key
member in promoting the growth of the company and enabling it to
cross its 100-year milestone.

Sharma began his formal education at St Joseph's Convent, Allahabad,
completing it at Mayo College, Ajmer, and graduating from the
University of Allahabad. He studied family business management at
SP Jain Institute, Mumbai, at the ripe age of thirty-five.

A leading name in healthcare, he is on the board of governors of the
Santokba Durlabhji Memorial Hospital, Jaipur, and is a founding
board member of Chaudhary Brahm Prakash Ayurved Charak
Sansthan, New Delhi. He is a recipient of the Nagarjuna Award,
the highest award in Ayurveda. He has also received the Superbrand
Award for Baidyanath Chyawanprash.

A passionate painter and a giver at heart, Sharma resides with his
family in New Delhi.

HOW TO THRIVE
IN A
FAMILY
BUSINESS

BUSINESS LESSONS
FROM MY
BAIDYANATH JOURNEY

AJAY SHARMA

PORTFOLIO
PENGUIN

An imprint of Penguin Random House

PORTFOLIO

USA | Canada | UK | Ireland | Australia
New Zealand | India | South Africa | China

Portfolio is part of the Penguin Random House group of companies
whose addresses can be found at global.penguinrandomhouse.com

Published by Penguin Random House India Pvt. Ltd
4th Floor, Capital Tower 1, MG Road,
Gurugram 122 002, Haryana, India

Penguin
Random House
India

First published in Portfolio by Penguin Random House India 2021

Copyright © Ajay Sharma 2021

ISBN 9780143454953

Typeset in Sabon by Digiultrabooks Pvt. Ltd
Printed at Replika Press Pvt. Ltd, India

www.penguin.co.in

MIX
Paper from
responsible sources
FSC® C016779

To my dear father,
Ram Avatar Sharma,
my guru

Contents

Quotes   *xi*
Foreword   *xiii*
Preface   *xv*

The Story behind the Book   1
Size of Family Businesses in India   6
The Journey of a Business: The Trimurti   9

The First Generation: Brahma   10
The Second Generation: Vishnu   10
The Third Generation: Mahesh   12

The Journey of a Generation: The Ashrams   15

The First Stage: Brahmacharya   21
The Second Stage: Grihastha   49
The Third Stage: Vanaprastha   111
The Fourth Stage: Sanyas   157

4 Ts: Train, Transact, Transition, Turn-in   167

Acknowledgements   173
Note from the Author   175
Disclaimer   177

'Mere change is not growth. Growth is the synthesis of change and continuity, and where there is no continuity, there is no growth.'

—C.S. Lewis

The 30 Sins

Sin 1: The elder son syndrome
Sin 2: Not nurturing early skills and talents
Sin 3: Staying in your comfort zone
Sin 4: Not networking with siblings/cousins who are your shareholders
Sin 5: Not endorsing early decision-making
Sin 6: Not providing clarity to your children over shareholding between siblings and cousins
Sin 7: Not building a good character
Sin 8: Not being exposed to higher education
Sin 9: Not spending time with spouse and children
Sin 10: Not identifying your passion and pursuing it
Sin 11: Delaying early division
Sin 12: Trying to fit into someone else's shoes
Sin 13: Following the 'If It Ain't Broke, Don't Fix It' principle
Sin 14: Burning yourself and not lighting up
Sin 15: Not acknowledging the importance of spouse
Sin 16: Allowing interference from the in-laws
Sin 17: Not creating a formal family charter
Sin 18: Getting the next generation to inherit conflict
Sin 19: Breaking away from the family charter/Going against the family charter
Sin 20: Not upgrading oneself
Sin 21: Not growing the pie
Sin 22: Not eliminating secondary conflicts
Sin 23: Not realizing the dawn of Vanaprastha

Sin 24: Not being ready to let go or reluctance in handing over the management

Sin 25: Not moving towards professionalization in the third generation

Sin 26: Letting the circles completely overlap or be mutually exclusive

Sin 27: Not having a succession plan

Sin 28: Not having a family office

Sin 29: Not having an exit policy

Sin 30: Not relinquishing ownership

'What I have found is that, in a family business structure, sometimes what is needed is a sense of discipline rather than creativity. You have to take everyone's ideas and make them work. When you are dealing with money, there is a limitation on how creative you can be.'

—**Ashwin Sanghi**

'When our family business separation was implemented, as the eldest member of the family, I had taken the entire burden of debts. I believe it was my mistake to have told myself, "Subhash, you can earn and repay the creditors".'

—**Subhash Chandra**

'When I took over the family business, it had already been a publicly traded company for twenty years. During one of the first annual meetings I attended, one shareholder stood up and advised me and everyone in attendance that I should resign.'

—**Azim Premji**

'I had the option of building a career in the US. Many of my friends who went there at the time did not come back, but for me, building the family business and being with family was worth coming back. I became a general manager within four months as I used my education to improve productivity and output.'

—**Baba Kalyani**

'When I was eighteen, and entered my family business, I soon realized that it wasn't as easy as I thought. I had to deal with people of my father's generation. Building trust was key to doing business.'

—**Binod Chaudhary**

'I was not very keen on joining the family business ... there were fourteen family members working together, and it worried me that I would not have enough individuality.'

—**Uday Kotak**

FOREWORD

Two classic proverbs come to mind:

> *Lessons from history, if not grasped, will be repeated till learnt.*

> *One who learns from mistakes is intelligent. But one who learns from the mistakes of others is wise.*

Transition is always difficult. We have always experienced it in some form or another. It is even more difficult in business, especially family-owned ones involving intergenerational transition and intragenerational rebalancing to maintain equilibrium.

This book addresses these twin issues within the very interesting edifice—the four stages of life—from the ancient shastras. Predominantly, for Indian-owned family businesses, this transition is not just difficult, but also painful, both financially and emotionally. The resultant losses are not only monetary, but also familial.

I have known Ajay for more than thirty years now. So, I have had the privilege of viewing, first-hand, the experiences he narrates in the book. He offers a bird's eye view to the reader on how to run a business that is 100 years old; ways to maintain balance between work and family while navigating through the four stages of life—Brahmacharya, Grihastha, Vanaprastha and Sanyas; how to be firm in business dealings when there could be family members with different opinions; on nurturing early talent and skills; and staying ahead of the times in terms of technology and education, etc.

One can see the honest, earnest and straight off-the-bat approach typical of Ajay's writings. The uncomplicated language, clear articulation of thought and precise suggestions, with pointers from Ajay based on his personal experience on how to avoid committing the sins, as well as opinions of well-established business leaders managing family businesses, provide an interesting opportunity for vicarious learning. The relevance of the contents at a time of constant churn is unquestionable.

We have all experienced, either directly or indirectly, the development of close-knit relationships not just among siblings but also the extended cousin group in the initial stages of life; followed by the discovery of competing interests and unique individual responses of the very same people on entry into business. Ajay is a fine example of how strong family values enable a young mind to deal with, and balance, the inevitable tussle between individual aspirations and the greater good. The ability to grasp the unsaid, reach out to the unsettled and carry everyone along, for the benefit of all are the fine qualities that Ajay displays in his dealings with stakeholders in business.

The book is a reflection of the continuing transition that the Baidyanath Group embraces while nurturing leaders of the next generation. I, as a first generation professional, could easily relate to the 'four' stages in which professional or business life has been captured in the book. I am sure others, whether from the first, second or third generation, will relate to and enjoy reading the book as much as I have.

—Vivek Kohli
Advocate General of Sikkim

PREFACE

My tryst with entrepreneurship started when I didn't even realize what it meant. Being born into a business family doesn't guarantee that you'll grow up to be a successful entrepreneur. Rather it is how your parents influence you; early age training; one's learnings from social surroundings and the experience you gain from exposure, that make you who you are.

This story was buried somewhere deep at the back of my mind. I'm glad I remembered it eventually. It has made introspection, and the journey of writing this book, all the more enjoyable.

It begins in Allahabad. During one of those sweaty summers, the gang of kids, including me, decided to do a series of short plays that the rest of the family would pay to watch. The objective of orchestrating the entire performance was to earn extra cash that could be spent on ice-cream cones and candies, a delight during summers. I must confess, before I begin, that I wasn't the leader of the group nor was the idea completely mine. It was an outcome of the joint efforts of future CEOs and presidents of multi-crore companies. What I did and still do take credit for is the right marketing and expansion strategy that I adopted for it.

We started off play season with assured customers—our family members—who we knew would come because they loved us. They were loyal customers. We performed, and the family loved it. They wanted us to repeat the performance because they found it cute. At that point, it was I who took the lead and said that we would re-enact the play, but it would cost them.

Since they were returning customers, we would offer them discounts but they had to pay up for an encore. I didn't understand business jargon or its terminologies then, but I understood its pulse. The family readily agreed, and we started rehearsing again. We worked on variations in the storyline to make it more interesting, so that they could keep coming back for more. Meanwhile, we also heard our elders boast about the series of short plays to neighbours. They were marketing it for us. Sensing an opportunity there, we advertised it to neighbours and involved their kids by giving them roles in the modified version of the play. That made the play even more appealing to them and we managed to get a bigger audience.

Was that entrepreneurship? Could I have been declared an entrepreneur for pulling that off with my siblings and friends? If we go by the popular definition of an entrepreneur—someone taking risks to earn profits—I don't think I could really be called one.

However, from my perspective, the answer to the question as to who is an entrepreneur and who isn't, remains very simple but is layered. It starts with the desire to create something—be it for profit or not for-profit. The second, after desire, is the ability to grab the opportunity by its throat. The next layer is the fine execution of the said opportunity and its strategic expansion. The fourth layer is to keep it going in the long run.

Apart from the layers addressed above, the business or perhaps the venture per se, needs to have a unique element which addresses a gap or otherwise stands out from existing competitors. You might just start selling the same product that ten other businesses have been selling, but if your marketing strategy stands out or let's say the pricing is far better, you are just as much an entrepreneur as anyone pushing a completely new product.

After the play, we finally divided the money amongst ourselves; to be frank, it is difficult to define exactly what I felt. All I can say is that I felt satisfied. But it was not the same satisfaction that you get after passing an exam by studying hard or the contentment of scoring a hundred on hundred.

The intensity of satisfaction was far beyond that because it was not 'my' achievement, but 'ours'. It was right in front of me and I could touch it, and feel it. It was an accomplishment by our family comprising siblings, cousins, relatives and friends, who actually pooled in their talents; stood committed towards a shared vision; had fun and enjoyed the act; basked in their individual recognitions and collectively shared the accolades and earnings. Isn't that what we call a family business? You can live it if you have the desire to.

Apart from such encounters of early 'entrepreneurship', another thing which eventually helped me successfully run the business was the feeling that I was somehow connected to the business. I credit my father for this. He openly discussed business at home and made me feel that I was part of it very early on. Thus, I developed a passion for our family business, Baidyanath, that has expanded to become a Rs 700-crore brand today.

My mother firmly believed in alternative medicine. Therefore, we received ayurvedic and homeopathic treatments. This introduced us to our products at a very young age. I distinctly recall a Baidyanath medicine that the children of the household were to consume every day. It certainly didn't appeal to our sweet-devouring palate. I received praise and sighs of relief from my siblings when I mixed crushed sugar to it in just the right proportions; making it more palatable for us.

All through life, I have been an innovator, a keen observer and a student at heart, learning heavily from my experiences and, importantly, from the experiences of others. I clearly remember it was the year 2008, some twelve years ago, when I had the yearning to compile my acquired wisdom. Out of an impulse, I started penning them down. To be honest, again, I did not clearly envisage what the end result would be. These learnings became the foundation; my starting point for all further research on the subject of 'family businesses'.

On one hand, business is an economic unit, the operations and management of which have developed into a science and are being taught in B-schools across the globe. The family, on the other hand, is a social unit that might be living together because of a common ancestry, but working separately and independently. A family business is unique because it is joined together by virtue of the common ancestry and the fact that its members also work together in business. One can find this model everywhere, from a large business corporation to the corner *kirana* store. What is so different about it then? Why is a family business such a complex unit? When a group of youngsters like us could have had fun and earned from a play, why can't adults enjoy living together and earning from a business? The most apparent difference is that we belonged to the same age group and the same generation. A family business comprises people from multiple generations, at times up to four, living under the same roof and working for a common business, making for a complex ecosystem called a family business.

Having worked in a 100-year-old family business myself, I have seen businesses behave as per the behaviour of the generation that manages it. My first-hand experience demonstrates that given an identical situation, the decision would vary as per the generation taking the call. Subsequent studies on the phenomena and research of more than 250 family businesses made me a proponent of the 'Generation Dimension'. I explain it as an analogy between the Trimurti of the Hindu pantheon and the different generations of a family business.

Life is all about the choices we make. The decisions we make become 'virtues' for the family and the business if they turn out to be right. If not, they become 'sins'.

All businesses and families are faced with situations that are unique to them. For solutions, they rely on available theories, templates and matrices based on research carried out on family businesses. They may find their answers in collaboration with advisers, consultants; their CAs, or lawyers who help them with 'what to do'.

How to Thrive in a Family Business is an attempt to highlight what every member and every generation of a family ought not to do. I trust every reader will relate to parts of my journey, regardless of which stage they are at, in their family business. I have identified thirty actions which are the biggest sins that hinder prosperity and continuity of business. I hope that this book will be helpful to everyone—not just stakeholders of family businesses, but also the millions who work with these family businesses, people who are the real lifeforce behind a company, who need to understand their environment. I believe this book will bring about a better understanding and help shareholders and employees, collectively, to sustain the business for generations to come. Before we move on to reading and grasping the gravity of the sins, it is important for the reader to understand:

Journey of a Business—The Trimurti: A business is started by one generation and owned and managed by subsequent generations. The business experiences three distinct behavioural patterns of the first, second and third generations, a concept that is discussed in detail in the book.

Journey of a Generation—The Ashrams: Each generation has a lifecycle. This generation dimension is best explained by the fours Ts—a micro study of the stages of each generation.

The concept of PRIME conflicts is another attempt to focus on the five core issues that plague a family business.

I sincerely hope that the book is a guide for the larger good of the thousands of family businesses and their younger generations who are going to own and run it. I hope the reader will take advantage of these learnings and experiences and leverage them keeping in mind the current environment of a growing economy. Can Indian family businesses thrive, go global, or will the family be a roadblock to it?

THE STORY BEHIND THE BOOK

December 2017

I was attending the wedding of the son of one of Baidyanath's big-league distributors. After addressing the overwhelming hellos and namastes of people who knew me, or just wanted to exchange pleasantries, I located a quiet seat away from the main festivities. I had just pulled out my phone to check a few emails.

I suddenly heard a 'Hello . . .' from someone standing close. I looked up, all set to greet the person with a gleaming smile. It was a young man in his early twenties whom I could not recall. Although that didn't matter, really. I greeted him with a powerful handshake, and he took a seat next to me. Lean, with a tux on his person, he sported a messy hairdo and a know-it-all look. Must be a fresh MBA grad, I thought.

'I heard you are writing a book . . . on Baidyanath . . .' he inquired. I was amazed. Not many people knew that I was working on a book.

'Not on Baidyanath per se. I am writing about my journey. And family businesses,' I told him.

'Oh really? But what's so new about that?' he asked with uneasy confidence.

'You should wait till the book is finished to find out,' I replied cleverly, in a snap.

'Give me a crash course. I mean, what really does a family business mean to you?'

His question sounded almost like a request. I wasn't sure why I would do that in the middle of a wedding with two urgent mails to reply to. But the thirst in his eyes was enough to transform me from a business owner into a writer/author. The purpose of the book—sharing what I knew came back to me instantly on seeing his eagerness. Maybe the kid could contribute a bit to it?

'To understand what a family business is, you first need to understand what family and business mean independently...'

I quickly grabbed a tissue in front of me and took a pen from my pocket. I unfolded the tissue and put it on the table while the kid watched. I drew a circle on it first.

'... This is family. It is a unit of people who are together for sustenance,' I told him. And then I drew another circle near it.

'This other circle is business. It is the system that will give the family this sustenance.' And then, I drew two circles overlapping each other. Set A is family, set B is business.

'In a family business, while set A takes care of set B and set B takes care of set A, both take care of each other, and yet, they have individual identities and aspirations. It's all about to what extent they depend on each other, it's all about the healthy overlap,' I told him excitedly.

Figure 1

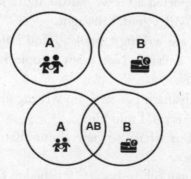

Where:
A = Family
B = Business
AB = Family managing the business

'But how much of this overlap is healthy? Do you have an equation?' the Einstein-in-disguise asked me. The kid is amusing as well as intelligent, I thought to myself.

'No, there is no equation. Life is not all mathematics...' I said with authority. 'The overlap can increase or decrease depending on the overall situation or the generation that is running the family business. If the area of overlap is higher that means a greater number of family members are engaged in the management of the business. If the area of overlap is small, it implies that a lesser number of family members are engaged in the business. This intersection area of AB has to be optimized and should not be too small or too big for sustainable functioning of the family business. It depends on variables like the generation managing the business, the aspirations of the individual family units, the personal needs of each member and the financial expectations of the owners,' I concluded.

'Can I keep this paper?' he asked innocently and stood up. I nodded, and he picked up the paper and left.

I am not sure how much he learned from me, but he surely helped me realize that there are a large number of micro-, small- and medium-sized businesses run by families who have barely any understanding of the concept called family business. Be it the intricacies of managing the family and the business, as well as watching over the influence of the overlap of both, there is little direction on crisis avoidance, leave alone the concept of crisis management.

The Third Set

Set A, set B and the intersection of the two sets (AB) have evolved into a more profound theory based on three sets. It introduces the importance of ownership. Though applicable to all family businesses, its relevance is greater in second- and third-generation businesses, businesses being operated by professionals, or families like ours that have moved from the siblings' stage to the cousins' stage. The set A, B and C theory was developed by Renato Tagiuri and John Davis. It is very helpful in defining the role of each family member, which is crucial for crisis management.

Figure 2

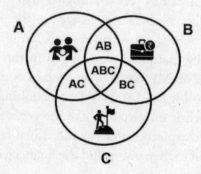

Where:
A = Family
B = Business
C = Ownership (equity)

AB = Family in business, but does not have ownership
AC = Family has ownership, but not managing
BC = A non-family owner in business
ABC = A family member who is an owner and manages the business

Instead of one intersection of AB, this diagram introduces four intersections between three sets. When families start expanding and the numbers start growing, one should map all stakeholders—the family, the owner and the business manager—on to the diagram. It is then that a clear picture emerges on who belongs where. Each set or intersection area is the defined boundary within which each member has to operate. The power, the position, the communication hierarchy, all start falling into place. This is the basic tool, a perfect start for larger families to manage a business with healthy interpersonal relationships. Typically, families include all members in the decision-making process on every issue concerning the family. To avoid crises, the three-set theory defines boundaries, and recommends that members be kept out of decisions that do not directly impact them.

SIZE OF FAMILY
BUSINESSES IN INDIA

How big is a family business? Before we get down to discussing the sins, let's take a stab at the scale of family businesses in India.

Fifteen of the top twenty business groups in India in 2016 were family-owned. Together, they controlled assets worth nearly Rs 26 lakh crore (USD 390 billion) at the end of FY16, accounting for 84 per cent of combined assets of the top twenty business groups. They generated revenue worth Rs 18 lakh crore in FY16, accounting for 80 per cent of the sample combined revenue, demonstrating resilience in the face of dramatic changes in the economy since Independence.

The contribution of family businesses to the national economy has been exceptional. Over the past two decades, the performance of family-controlled businesses has been superior than either government, or publicly, owned companies. At least half of the Nifty 50 firms on the National Stock Exchange (NSE) are family-controlled. If you take the top 500 firms on the Bombay Stock Exchange (BSE), 73 per cent of them are family-controlled. And that percentage rises if you include medium-sized firms.

As per data collected in 2019, Farhad Forbes, current chairman of Family Business Network (FBN) International, an organization to network business families to share, learn and collaborate to prolong the lifespan of their businesses, says that globally as well as in India, family businesses contribute over 70 per cent of Gross Domestic Product (size of economy) of most developing and developed countries. In India, it could be even higher because almost every small enterprise is family-run.

From a global perspective, here is a quick glance at the contribution of family businesses to their national GDPs in 2016:

+ Mexico (90 per cent)
+ Brazil (85 per cent)
+ United Kingdom (70 per cent)
+ Malaysia (67.2 per cent)
+ Spain & China (65 per cent)
+ France, Portugal, Colombia (60 per cent)
+ United States (57 per cent)
+ Belgium, Germany (55 per cent)

The Centre for Family Business at University of St Gallen, Switzerland, along with the EY Global Family Business Centre of Excellence, compiled the Global Family Business Index in 2015. The top 500 family businesses in the world contributed USD 6.5 trillion to global GDP in 2013—more than the combined contributions of the French and German economies. While the revenue was more than half compared to Fortune 500 companies (USD 12.2 trillion); when it came to employment numbers, the number of employees hired by the top 500 family businesses was two-thirds higher (24.6 million people).

Irrespective of geographical locations and different cultures, family businesses hold sway everywhere and are very much a part of the world's economy. India ranks third globally in terms of number of family-owned businesses with 111 companies that have a total market capitalization of USD 839 billion. China, with 159 firms, and the United States, with 121 firms, are in first and second positions, says a report.[1]

The abovementioned ranking of Indian firms changes when we take into consideration average size. The Indian companies that were studied are more mature, with 60 per cent among those family businesses in their third generation as compared to China and the US. While this ranking should make us feel proud, the fact that a majority of family businesses do not cross the third generation is a sign of caution. We Indians are far more emotional and let feelings drive our actions when it comes to decision-making. And the higher the stakes, the higher emotions tend to run. Particularly in larger joint families, it is difficult to separate emotions, when distant family members join the business and try to influence it in their own ways—right there is the scope for a situation to turn it into a total disaster.

THE JOURNEY OF A
BUSINESS: THE TRIMURTI

A business behaves or responds as per the generation that is managing it. Yes, the generation managing the business becomes a critical factor when we analyse its journey. Why does a generation have such an important role to play in business behaviour and response? How does each generation impact the business?

Structures and boundaries don't make an organization. It is the group of people within it that do. Their collective vision is honed in accordance with the leader in control at that moment. A prime minister leads a country, a CEO heads a company, a general leads an army. Be it an institution, organization, company, or a country, the leadership is the face that projects the organization. They are leaders because they can be followed. Their leadership style—be it charismatic, authoritative, affiliative, or transformative—becomes the behavioural response of the organization. In a family business, we have owner–managers—they own and manage a business— the impact this leadership has on the business is far greater than that of a pure manager.

The way generations and businesses evolve is strikingly similar to the evolution of the world, as explained in our scriptures. The ancient wisdom of these scriptures has always fascinated me, and I still keep going back to them from time to time. I believe the knowledge and truth that you find there is reflected in all kinds of modern philosophies that we now invent and follow. Growing up in a family business steeped in Ayurveda, we value the wealth and knowledge present in these scriptures.

This led me to infer similarities between the creation of a family business and its subsequent generations, how they feel for, respond to and lead a business and the creation of the world itself and the Hindu trinity (trimurti) of Brahma (the creator), Vishnu (the preserver) and Mahesh/Shiva (the destroyer)[2].

This analogy helps one to understand the mindset and its resultant behavioural pattern of each generation and its impact on business. This is how, as I envisage it, the journey of a business with various generations progresses:

The First Generation: Brahma

Brahma created the world. In a family, the one who starts the business is Brahma. The first generation entrepreneur has a burning desire to be their own boss, for which they deploy all resources like time, money, effort and beliefs. They usually start solo and build a team of co-founders, investors and workers. This new entrepreneur is optimistic and puts everything at stake to achieve success, which may not be the case for subsequent generations for various reasons. They are dedicated and work hard to realize their passion; in most cases, their input is more than the output they derive out of the business due to a high fear of losing one's investment. Like Brahma, they create a new world of business—the foundation—for future generations to build on, and enjoy its fruits.

The Second Generation: Vishnu

Vishnu gracefully receives the created world and has the responsibility of preserving it by managing it right. Similarly, the second generation receives the world of business; their role is to ensure continuity through effective management practices.

---

2   The Trimurti is the trinity of supreme divinity in Hinduism through which the cosmic functions of creation, sustenance and destruction are personified. The triad of deities are Brahma the creator, Vishnu the preserver, and Shiva the destroyer.

Vishnu is well aware that He didn't create this world; it is already functional and there are people to manage it in a predefined way. Vishnu's role, too, is predefined as a preserver. The inheritors of the business are raised from childhood to preserve the legacy of the creator; a responsibility that requires them to be calm, to understand the business environment and be flexible about managing it. The successor knows that they are not the leader of the team and, in order to be one, they have to prove themselves. They become learners and problem-solvers who take on various forms (avatars) to enter the management or hand-hold the organization, as and when required.

Vishnu, the perfect 'owner–manager' rests on a Sheshanag (many-headed serpent) in the middle of a vast calm ocean with Saraswati (the goddess of knowledge) and Lakshmi (the goddess of wealth) as consorts by His side. What does this image communicate? If we observe and try to relate to it from a management point of view, this is what we can interpret:

1. **He lives in a calm ocean:** Vishnu lives in a calm ocean which signifies a calm environment—a pivotal element for effective decision-making. He lives away from the day-to-day chaos of the earth (read business) and executes decisions from His abode, thus expressing continuity and transparency. He stays away to encourage teamwork and independence of operations and accepts everyone's opinion when they approach Him, displaying the good leadership qualities of an owner–manager.

2. **He has the company of Saraswati and Lakshmi:** The presence of Saraswati (knowledge) is a mandate for Lakshmi (wealth) to stay, and Vishnu must balance both. It is also common knowledge that if Saraswati leaves, Lakshmi will leave too. Wealth only stays in places where knowledge exists. He works on His skills and knowledge to, first, retain and, subsequently, create more wealth. This helps Him foster clear and detailed communication. He rewards

publicly, thus making work enjoyable. He leads by example by involving Himself where He is needed—like the famous Ram and later Krishna avatars that He has donned as a discipline-enforcer, game-changer and solution-provider.

3. **He resides on Sheshanag:** Vishnu resides on Sheshanag, who is a mighty snake representing fear. Fear sets boundaries making managers aware of consequences. Hence, they approach Vishnu only when necessary, discouraging flattery and sycophancy by senior managers. Vishnu has a good feedback system of the world through Narad, His chief informer.

I personally consider this generation to be the most important one for a family business. Vishnu teaches us that the charisma and capability of the creator should not be a burden on the second generation as they don't have to create a new world; instead, they should have the skills to preserve the business legacy. Building a car or a computer requires skills that are different from those required for operating it. In a business context, preserving or managing means growing the business. If there is stagnation in the business, it is not being managed well. Hence, the second generation can enjoy the fruits of labour of the first one only if it can manage and grow well.

What's important to highlight is that the characteristics of Vishnu defined here aren't exclusive to Him. For sure, they have a stronger significance associated with Him and hence are symbolically credited to Him. However, the need for solid management abilities holds true for all generations.

The Third Generation: Mahesh

When the world needed the holy water of the Ganga but was not ready to bear her weight, it was Mahesh who received it in His hair and gave it to the world. He controls the river, sits on top of the mountain and oversees everything. He drinks poison so that the world can sustain.

He is usually calm and non-interfering. Among the trinity, He is the one who is known to enjoy the company of His family, and encourage the children to succeed individually and develop individual identities. He promotes His children on the basis of merit and not seniority. He also has a third eye—the capacity to see beyond the obvious. The third eye is also the eye of wisdom gathered over the past two generations. But, at the same time, He has a volatile side. The side that can destroy the world (business). The side which, if provoked, will perform a taandav (the dance of destruction) and destroy every inch of it. So, while Brahma creates the world and Vishnu manages it, Mahesh/Shiva, who represents the third generation, has the potential to destroy it. The Shiva–Shankar personalities can be seen in the third, fourth, fifth and subsequent generations. All of them have the potential to destroy and are hence Mahesh.

How can it be ensured that He doesn't destroy it? Do not upset Him. Don't make Him angry since He does not get upset on His own. There are external factors that make Him angry. It is Mahesh who bears the weight of the continuity of the business, or its ultimate destruction. I am the third generation. I am Mahesh in a 100-year-old family business with multiple generations and a large number of family members. This book offers my perspective on the multiple dynamics that impact a family business through the generations of creator, preserver and destroyer. The sins they must avoid in their journey of life, which is distinctively divided into four stages discussed as ashrams.

Am I Mahesh? I have often asked myself this question.

My father used to have a lot of visitors at the family house. We had businessmen, politicians, bureaucrats, academics, artists, and film stars come over. They were achievers in their field, and we used to hear their stories.

I often heard a couple of things more than others:

'Ram, you have four sons, you must plan,' a bureaucrat friend of my father would tell him.

'Ram Bhai, what have you planned for the future of your four sons?' an affluent neighbour would question.

'Ram, 80 per cent of family businesses collapse in the third generation.' A close family friend, belonging to the second generation himself, told him.

It was then that I thought of the analogy of Brahma, Vishnu and Mahesh that I just explained. And, after listening to all the suggestions and words of caution from well-wishers, I felt a certain amount of responsibility.

Mahesh is sitting calmly in the Himalayas; controlling the river. He is ensuring the continuity of life; He wants peace and prosperity. He is doing what needs to be done for the world to live. But yes, if you provoke Him, don't give Him His dues, He might destroy everything, by doing the taandav. So, while He does everything in His power to sustain continuity, He still carries the label of a destroyer because He has the potential to destroy.

So is the third generation to which I belong, really a destroyer? No, I don't think they are born to destroy. Does clear communication and business transparency reduce by the time the third generation enters the business environment or are there other factors which can be a cause for provocation? Certainly there ought to be answers. I was aware of families which had flourished through their third generation.

This shaped my working style. I understood that though my generation could spoil what the previous two generations had built and managed, there was a methodology to avoid it. This is that curse which every family business in the world is still living with. And it used to haunt me. The more I used to hear or read about it, the more it used to burden me with responsibility. I wanted to break the curse.

THE JOURNEY OF A
GENERATION: THE ASHRAMS

Before we get on to the journey of how the curse was broken in our case, let's first acknowledge that each generation has a similar life cycle. The journey of every generation has four stages, defined through this book as the 4 Ts of life. Understanding these stages within a particular generation and managing them right is part of breaking the curse.

Since the impact of a generation on the behaviour and response of a business is strong, it is important to minutely study the generations. Doesn't a person change with age? Don't some people evolve with time and experience? Not just physically but also intellectually and emotionally? So, within the generation, there are phases which need to be analysed independently.

In the way that the three generations are symbolically Brahma, Vishnu and Mahesh, every generation has a life cycle which is analogous with what is defined in *Dharma Shastra*. As per the scriptures, individual human life goes through four categorical stages, defined as (see Figure 3):

1. Brahmacharya
2. Grihastha
3. Vanaprastha
4. Sanyas

It is fascinating how these four stages are identical to what one goes through in their journey with the family business. Let's understand this better.

Brahmacharya is the first stage of one's life; the initial years spent in acquiring skills, knowledge and nurturing talent. Broadly speaking, this phase of one's life should be spent on overall education, development and the **training** of a person. **T1**

After Brahmacharya, we all face the challenges of the real world. Welcome to Grihastha. You join or start a business; you may marry to start a family. The **transaction** of life begins with the creation of wealth. **T2**

Post Grihastha, you will enter Vanaprastha which is the stage where you are preparing the next generation to manage and hand over the functions to them. In effect, you are planning your own **transition**. **T3**

Finally, it is Sanyas (the stage of renunciation), the time to retire. This is when you hand over the complete management, help ownership transition from one generation to another, and in the process, fully secure yourself for the **turn-in**. **T4**

You have heard about the 4 Ps of marketing by E. Jerome McCarthy.

Now understand the 4 Ts of life in a family business that I have created for generations to follow:

Training
Transaction
Transition
Turn-in

Let's take a look at these various stages, defined as the 'Ts of a generation in the family business' and how they manifest when we talk about ongoing generations of a family owning a business. How owners can avoid sins and ensure continuity to reap dividends of the business for the family, provide for the needs arising in all stages of life like education and marriage for the young, ensure status and comfortable standards of living for adults and medical expenses and care for the elderly are all addressed here. The sole intent being peace, harmony and happiness within the family.

Figure 3

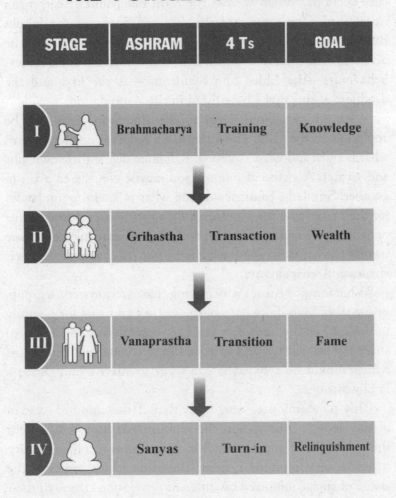

THE 4 STAGES OF ASHRAM

STAGE	ASHRAM	4 Ts	GOAL
I	Brahmacharya	Training	Knowledge
II	Grihastha	Transaction	Wealth
III	Vanaprastha	Transition	Fame
IV	Sanyas	Turn-in	Relinquishment

Before we move through each generation (the Brahma, Vishnu and Mahesh) of a family and their stages, let's begin with the family as an entity. While individual behaviour is a widely discussed topic, generational behaviour will be taken up in later sections. When we use the term behaviour, it can mean rituals, rules, customs and the dos and don'ts of the family. But for the scope of this discussion, let's limit ourselves to the business behaviour of a family. One of the most natural business behaviours—the Elder Son Syndrome—is the first and the deadliest of sins that I have listed in this compilation.

What is considered a sin in the Ramayana may not be applicable to the Gita. The latter has a different connotation of what is right and what is wrong. Religions define their own sins and virtues. A virtue of one religion maybe considered a sin in another. Similarly, countries decide what is lawful or unlawful for their citizens. Ethnic groups follow their own cultural norms on what to do and what not to do and families inculcate in their members what is right and what is wrong. All clearly define what virtues and what sins are.

What is a sin? An act which brings harm to a system, a group, or a goal is a sin. So what are the virtues and sins for a family business? I am no authority but I have made a sincere effort to share my knowledge and experiences in identifying thirty sins which should be avoided if you want to survive and thrive a family business.

This pandemic has taught us that if the immune system of the body is healthy and the immunity is high, it can fight the onslaught of any disease. Family business is a living entity, it has its own immune system. The virus attack comes in the shape of sins, committed by different generations through their four stages of life. There are different variants which affect in childhood, adulthood, midlife and old age. Businesses which succumb get destroyed. How can one build immunity within a family business? There are actions of individuals or the family unit which reduce the immunity and make the family business susceptible to the curse. These sins must be avoided so that they don't infect the body. A healthy family sustains a long-lasting family business. There are lessons to be learnt in each sin. Readers can take these learnings and apply them with ease.

Sin 1: The Elder Son Syndrome

India has largely been an agrarian country. Our customs, festivals and common rituals are connected to agriculture and have given rise to the concept of the elder son being the obvious heir or the next family supreme to take charge.

Since the elder one gains strength first, he also becomes the responsible one since agriculture is about strength and muscle. It is years and years of mental conditioning that has defined the way we think and live and given power to the eldest male member in the household.

With the prevalence of the Hindu Undivided Family (HUF) system in India, the importance of the elder male found further prominence. An HUF or a joint family is one single entity with social status and economic power. If the head passes away, an undesirable vacuum is created which may put the HUF in disarray. Hence, as per seniority, the eldest male is the head of the family and *karta* of the HUF. The year 2005 witnessed the amendment to Section 6 of the Hindu Succession Act of India, giving full rights to daughters to be part of their father's HUF. We have witnessed this change of mindset after forty-nine years.

Furthermore, India has been a land of kings and queens. We have all grown up listening to inspirational stories of valour and sacrifice of these kings and queens. It is in our DNA to revere them, and, in extreme cases, worship and follow their actions. Centuries of conditioning, even as recent as being ruled by the British Crown, have instilled these beliefs. For luxury and lifestyle, business families and the elite, till today, look up, aspire and get influenced by royal families. Their succession plan is the same—the eldest of the male heirs inherits the throne.

This behaviour of business families, in my opinion, is a sin. For successful succession in business, one has to shun the elder son syndrome. Business families are already changing and the most talked about example is that of renowned industrialist G.D. Birla. He had three sons. The jewel companies of his empire were handed over to his grandson, Aditya Birla. Whatever may have been the internal reasons, the move paved the way for business families to think differently. They could see that his choice was clear—business first.

From agriculture to monarchy, there are varied deep-set influences which we carry into the business environment. We moved from our agricultural roots to business, but our mindset didn't. While agriculture is about strength, business is about a sharp mind. While the HUF is about continuity, business is about competency. While monarchy is about a figurehead, business is about leadership and vision; and hence, the mindset of considering the eldest as the natural successor/supreme doesn't find place here. The family must have a succession direction and not be glued to the obsolete order that is followed in agriculture or monarchy. In fact, one can see changes happening in royal families too. The reasons could be gender equality or other things, but laws are already being amended. Are these signals? The Succession to the Crown Act 2013 (an act of the Parliament of the United Kingdom) allows the eldest child—either male or female—to be the heir to the crown!

A successor in a family business must be competent to sustain the business and the family. He could be a family member or not. If we go by the elder son syndrome, we won't be able to place the most deserving person (or the right fit) in the leadership position. Hence, a departure from the elder son syndrome is essential and becomes the first indication that business families are serious about growth and continuity.

***

Brahmacharya T1:
Figure 4

FIRST STAGE

STAGE	ASHRAM	4 Ts	GOAL
I	Brahmacharya	Training	Knowledge
II	Grihastha	Transaction	Wealth
III	Vanaprastha	Transition	Fame
IV	Sanyas	Turn-in	Relinquishment

I don't remember too much of my childhood. It keeps coming back to me in bits and pieces when I let my mind wander into the wilderness of the unknown. Despite that, when I reach out to those memories, I know that they have significantly shaped me, my life, my business, my family and my family business. One such memory—the starkest of all that I remember—is the one where I got caught playing marbles by my mother.

I was squatting in the courtyard, within the walls of our house in Allahabad, and letting my fingers do their magic with the marbles. The household staff were following my game and showering me with appreciation through 'oohs' and 'aahs'. I was the focal point of the game, and I liked it that way. I remember my mother, clad in her blue saree, coming out through the main door for an unannounced inspection. The staff dispersed within seconds, but I was too engrossed in calculating my next move. She appeared right in front of me and asked me to get up. I did so, apologetically.

The next thing I knew, she had got on the telephone with Krishna Aunty, the wife of our general manager, who was her confidante and adviser explaining my act of dishonour in granular detail. Krishna Aunty proclaimed: 'Sons of kings are taught archery, not the art of playing with marbles.'

Even my mother, who was not from a business family, clearly knew what kids of a business family were supposed to do. Back then, though she was never introduced to the business, she knew the role she was supposed to play in the family business: raising her children right. It had to be so to ensure that they became the right successors for the legacy to be continued and expanded. While we will talk more about the difference between becoming a successor or a successor managing the business (SMB) and what role each member plays in a business family, let's go back to the time when I was caught playing marbles. Following the incident and to instil a sense of discipline in me, I was immediately packed off to a boarding school in the hills of Nainital.

However, upon our arrival, my mother rejected the school in Nainital outright. She was precise about the role of good food in the mental and physical development of a child, and no risks could be taken in that department. The school did not meet her quality standards. You see, all children are special and can achieve what they want to on their merit and more. But her children (I won't go to the length of saying extra special) though, had to be raised more cautiously. They were already entitled to something. If they were brought up right, trained well and set in the right direction, they could help in creating enormous value and wealth. I won't mention much about what could happen otherwise but there were all kinds of possibilities. Hence, the extra care and caution.

A very visible trait of the second generation. While their focus is on how to successfully sustain and grow the business, they look at the next generation as an important source of talent for the business. They nurture their children for management and business leadership roles that can contribute to the growth of the business, besides providing them with career options, in the same way their fathers paved the way for their entry into the family business. Contrary to this, the priority of the first generation is always towards building a business. The focus on the child, if at all, will be second or third on their priority list.

The next school on my mother's list was the Modern School in Delhi, and so we promptly arrived at the capital at my Nana's (maternal grandfather) home. We had had a long and exhausting day of completing procedures and formalities at Modern School. Later that evening, one of mother's uncles came calling at dinner. He was a professor at Mayo College in Ajmer. He sang praises of Mayo—the Eton of the East—and how it was THE school for the best of families, including the royals. My mother, however, was sold on the idea only when he said that they grew all food ingredients organically on farms within the school premises. This decision of my parents ensured that I got the right skills and training in the right environment.

Children from all business families must be trained for the future; not preparing them to be good owners becomes one of the earliest sins in our compilation.

Sin 2: Not Nurturing Early Skills and Talents

Early training is the foundation for cognitive and social development. Most successful people start early. Be it sports, arts, technology or any other field, starting early has its advantages. Innumerable examples come to mind. Sachin Tendulkar, Mark Zuckerberg, Lata Mangeshkar, Cristiano Ronaldo, A.P.J. Abdul Kalam and many more such achievers, have proven that early skill development—even if you have inherent talent—is the key to success.

Skill is an ability to do something. When this ability is developed further, one can execute better to deliver improved results, thus becoming proficient in the skill. Talent is the ability to do something naturally. While early training in soft skills is recommended, early identification of talent is also necessary.

What soft skills should be nurtured in a child is up to the parents, but my experience says that learnability is the basic skill one requires to succeed in life. All through life, and, especially in family businesses, one should not be rigid and must be prepared to unlearn, and then relearn. Children with this basic skill are the most successful in their chosen fields.

In a family business, another skill that is very helpful to a child and something they *must* learn is empathy—to see things from the point of view of others. Empathy leads you to compassion and does not make you a bully. Being creative should also be a priority and must be treated at par with agility. Visualizing the future and pre-empting it, makes one a good planner and a problem-solver. Lastly, I recommend resilience. Setbacks and obstacles are a way of life and the power to bounce back again and again is very critical in a dynamic family business environment.

Consider the case of the Mahabharata—this saga has the answers to many situations arising in our life today. It is imperative to mention Kunti for being a wise mother-queen who requested that her children (the five young Pandavas) be imparted the same education and training as the other princes.

The Pandavas became great warriors not because they were born Pandavas but because they underwent early training. It was Kunti who created that opportunity for her children to get the right training, and learn and develop skill-sets in the right environment.

While some skills are acquired consciously through the right kind of training, some are acquired unconsciously owing to our environment and surroundings. I have observed that in a typical business family where you have house help, your child unconsciously learns the art of management, or to be precise, the art of dealing with people.

For example, a family business household employs staff to support them, or help them run the household smoothly. The help could be full-time or part-time. This allows the family to devote their own time to critical business matters. The child of the house follows instructions of say, an ayah (nanny), a cook or a driver. As he grows older, he starts questioning them and becomes a part of the decision-making process. He becomes part of the team. Over time, he starts delegating tasks to them. So essentially, he learns the art of managing a team of people from different departments.

But that's just a good start, an advantage that children from business families have. It doesn't mean that formal skills and training are not required. You can't assume that one day, your children will learn to manage everything perfectly without consistent training. They have to start early and get into the habit of constantly upgrading and adding skills to their repertoire all through their lives. Management and entrepreneurship are skills and art rolled in one. As sad as it may sound, you can't be born with them. The onus is upon the parents to consciously develop soft skills early and open their children's mind to learning throughout life.

In life, when there are two or more people with the same qualifications or hard skills, soft skills are the differentiator. While dealing with colleagues, competition or government officials, it's always the early skills which leave an impression. People who lose out on early skill development can feel inadequate. Some may hone the skills later, which we hear as 'experience has taught me', others just lose out in the competitive environment. To save one's child from feeling inadequate or being a loser, it's the responsibility of parents/guardians to not commit this sin.

Sin 3: Staying in Your Comfort Zone

While I couldn't go to Nainital for my education, this idyllic hill station, developed by the colonial British, still has a special place in my heart. It was our second home. My father would take a month off from work every year and we would all head to Nainital! It was his solace and practically nothing could stop him.

My time in Nainital helped me learn to fend for everything on my own in uncertain surroundings, unpredictable situations and amidst unknown people. It threw a new challenge my way to make a new city my own, adapt to it and live in it, for one month every year. During that month, we stayed out of our comfort zone; from our routine in Allahabad. Staying in your comfort zone is akin to being in a comfortable room, oblivious to what's going on outside. Familiar surroundings and routines make life easy and stress-free. One doesn't want to learn or do new things as it makes them uncomfortable. In fact, one starts to accept a false narrative of disliking anything that one has not been exposed to, making you an introvert. Expanding your comfort zone breaks mental barriers, pushes you to do new things and makes the mind strong and adaptable. My new experiences helped me discover my own capabilities and find out who I truly was.

While the British left India in 1947, some of them continued to live in a few pockets in the country where their cultural influences and norms were still prevalent through the sixties up to the mid-seventies; Nainital being one of them. The iconic Boat House Club, famous for its yachting facility, was a meeting point for people from all walks of life. One lazy afternoon, I remember meeting Peter Smetachek, a German by descent. After a brief conversation, we visited his house which looked like a butterfly museum. It was an amazing experience to see his collection of beautiful butterflies. This is just one of many encounters. I had several more that exposed me to a number of people pursuing a wide range of interests and hobbies, including the upliftment of the local population through various engagements. There's so much to choose from and to do! While travel is a great teacher, the exposure of living in a distant location enhances one's learnings. Getting exposed to people from different social, cultural and economic backgrounds makes you compassionate towards others.

In fact, the kind of confidence that you get after moving out of your physical comfort zone cannot be the same if you are a sheltered kid. You become more proactive and independent being out and away, while staying sheltered makes you reactive and dependent. That being said, generalizations of any kind are toxic nonetheless and it's just as possible that a sheltered kid does better, if trained right.

Later, my father purchased a home for himself in Nainital. It became an essential part of my life and my affection for this place has only increased with time. It is the place from where I have written this book with a tang of nostalgia and shots of introspection. Before we bought our own place, each year, the family stayed at the famous Grand Hotel—located on Mall Road—with the popular bookstore Narayans' within the compound. After a hectic daily schedule of horse-riding, yachting, row-boating and housie (another name for tombola), I would find myself walking into Narayans'. The owner took a keen interest in every customer including us young children, guiding us on what to pick, introducing us to various topics and, at times, allowing us to read at the store without buying the book when it was out of our budget. A trip to Nainital, even today, is never complete if I don't visit the store. Fifty years have passed since then and the store is now managed by the next generation of owners who are as dedicated. I would like to express my gratitude to the Tiwari family for their contribution in shaping my interest in books.

The second force that further pushed me out of my comfort zone came from Mayo, my boarding school in Ajmer. It had its own challenges that kept propelling me ahead. Unlike common perceptions, boarding schools have a very protected environment. The administration ensures that everyone follows a good routine, and takes care of all needs like lodging, food, travel, recreation and academics. Menus are pre-decided, activities planned to the last detail with separate uniforms for each and classes follow a strict schedule, so one really does not have to plan anything. The day is spent just being part of the routine. With every need taken care of, the boarding school experience shook me out of my emotional comfort zone. It made me independent and a risk-taker. I must mention that I stammer, but throughout my stay, not a single person ever ridiculed or looked down upon me because of my shortcoming. This support was what helped me overcome my initial fears and forge my way ahead with confidence.

Every person has a comfort zone in life where they perform to their fullest capacity and deliver with ease. They are sought after and appreciated, but the choice before them is whether to be good or great. Comfort zones usually give rise to stagnation. For example, if you have been working on one job for several years, functions become familiar after some time, and you are able to handle situations with ease since you have mastered the role. This is good but it is also seen as stagnation. It is important that you widen your horizons and become great, step out of your comfort zone and explore unknown territories—in short, maybe accept greater responsibilities, or change your workplace for better opportunities. Stepping outside your comfort zone will push you to improve your performance levels and help you to move up the ladder, achieving greater success.

What was new and challenging in the past becomes a comfort zone in the present. I admire my parents for constantly exposing me to newer challenges till it became a part of my personality and a way of life. I would have stayed in my comfort zone, which would have been a sin in the ever-dynamic environment of a family business.

Sin 4: Not Networking with Siblings/Cousins Who Are Your Shareholders

How would you define networking? Going to a business event or a high-end soirée where you try to initiate conversations over a cup of coffee or drinks? It was different for us. Our networking opportunities were created at a family get-together, during family functions, festivals and any other reason that would bring us together. It was such an important part of our lives where all the cousins would meet, that even the company board meetings were not spared. Cities kept changing, but the entire family kept coming together irrespective; be it Calcutta, Patna, Allahabad, Kanpur, Delhi, Jhansi, Jaipur or Nainital. The mode of travel was by road or mainly by rail as the fear of flying kept my father away from air travel.

As we like to remember it now—we grew up in the 'Howrah-Delhi Express' culture. It was a premier train in those days, chugging its way from Calcutta to Delhi and back. Our family frequently travelled on it as the train offered first-class AC coaches and en route, stopped at towns that either had our factories or homes of family members. Our family was so well-acquainted with the train and its staff—the coach attendants, ticket checkers, helpers, driver, etc., that it had practically become our family's personal courier service. Our staff would hand over packages that we wanted to send to different cities to the train staff. The amazing part was that if our staff, for some reason, could not collect a package, the train staff would personally deliver it home. This familiarity built a trust towards them and it became a boon for us.

Even if the elders were unable to attend these get-togethers, they ensured that at least all the children could take these train journeys and be together. They understood the importance of networking among cousins within our third generation. And these train journeys were an enjoyable part of growing up. They made us more independent and somewhere, a sense of being unstoppable crept in, at least in my mind.

Returning to the subject of networking, these get-togethers in different cities were our networking platforms. We would meet our cousins who were to become future business partners. Bonds of childhood last forever since they are nurtured on the foundation of innocence; not of logic, reason or possible transactions. You might just be two very opposite and diverse personalities, but there is a high probability of forming a close and unique bond during childhood. You just click, and that's it. There is no rhyme or reason to it. And since it is innocent, with no absolute give and takes, it allows you the freedom to just talk about anything under the sun, moon and the stars. You don't have to find a purpose for a conversation. You have a conversation because you happen to be together.

In a joint family which is a business family, these interactions and networking exercises play an important part. Developing a bond with your siblings and cousins with whom you are going to share the business eventually, helps you go a long way. It helps you understand each other and break the ice which is critical since you have to share the business with them in the future. Early age networking results in smooth transactions, discussions and debates over serious matters of business in the future.

When we would go on these vacations and get-togethers in different cities, it was not just the cousins that came together.

We also met each other's group of friends and developed a bond with them too! These friends could be our future business leads and an extended network that could help us find connections. These friends of cousins, in the event of a relationship crisis, also, act as communication links.

This highly regarded networking, for which people now invest millions, happened at no cost and at an age where the bond would be the strongest! We bonded with our business partners and potential business leads over a game of Monopoly, carrom, ludo, badminton, cricket, swimming, or rounds of Uno. Whether it was a conscious decision of the second generation will always remain a mystery, but what they ensured was ease of working together in the family business for the third generation of Baidyanath, which consisted not only of cousins but also second cousins.

However, now, times have changed and so have the ways in which things used to happen—for both good and bad. We don't have such family get-togethers now, and there is no networking happening at that level. Today, families are becoming nuclear; living separately has become a trend, paving the way for individualistic development of each child within the larger family.

Individual development focuses on enhancing the strengths and skills of a person, a very important aspect in the competitive world of today. Yet, parents still need to address this lack of networking amongst children of today, as this networking and bonding softens the otherwise harsh business communication in the future. This perhaps is the most obvious sin that must not be committed, especially when a family business reaches a stage when cousins begin to get involved, whether in the second or third generation. Eventually, committing this sin can potentially result in greater conflicts in the context of the continuity of business.

Sin 5: Not Endorsing Early Decision-Making

'The risk of a wrong decision is preferable to the terror of indecision.'—Maimonides (Spanish philosopher)

Taking a wrong decision is not a sin. It can be corrected. But not allowing your children to take decisions is indeed a sin. You must help your child develop this soft skill and guide them to take decisions. Tell them the pros and cons, present them with reality, set time limits to teach them not to overthink but to leave the decision-making to them. Parents need to build this capability.

While studying in a boarding school like Mayo, there were decisions to be made which could have short- or long-term implications. At the age of twelve, decision-making was syringed into your veins.

While it was easy to choose between a wide variety of sports and physical activities during the day, the evenings in Mayo had a more interesting line-up. One had to choose between going to a temple for the 'Om Jai Jagadeesh'³ aarti or going for contemplation (a fifteen-minute talk by a teacher or seniors on varied topics). For me, going to the aarti was the obvious choice, but my curiosity about contemplation created a conflict. I decided to explore the newer world of contemplation while still sticking to my roots. I enrolled myself in contemplation. After the contemplation session, the god-fearing person that I was, I would rush to the temple and perform my rituals alone, before arriving at the mess, out of breath, for dinner. This arrangement could not last long. A choice had to be made. In the end, I chose the contemplation sessions over the aarti.

The decision-making didn't end there. At the mess, you had to decide if you wanted to be strictly vegetarian (we used to call them *parhezi*s), be a meat-eater or an eggetarian (a vegetarian who eats eggs but no meat)! At home, we normally had egg for breakfast, a strictly vegetarian lunch and, sometimes, meat for dinner.

---

³ A religious song sung to pay obeisance to Lord Vishnu.

At Mayo, you had to make a choice and live with it for the entire term. I became an 'eggetarian', a term my children always find funny.

There is so much to explore at a residential school—not just regarding food, but in relation to culture, behaviour and understanding of the world. You start seeing the world from different viewpoints which widens your own horizon of thinking and helps you make more informed decisions.

While I have emphasized how the boarding school helped me find my identity, I won't say that it is a thumb rule to send your kids to a boarding school! You might be surprised to read this, but while I speak so highly of going to a boarding school, I didn't send my children to one. But at the same time, I made them take early-life decisions and didn't impose. I guided them instead. The idea is to take the essence and learn; not to replicate. Every human being is different and so is every situation. We must act accordingly to walk on the path optimized uniquely for us.

Now, what this independence in decision-making brings up is an interesting question. Why exactly should you be independent to make a decision? It's because you not only inculcate leadership qualities but also become a problem-solver. That is a very important quality to have when you are working together in a family business. The challenge with decision-making is having the courage to either wait for the optimal solution or go ahead with the adequate one. Most people become habitual in either maximizing solutions or being satisfied early. To become an effective decision-maker, I recommend evaluation of each situation in order to be able to take an informed decision on whether to go optimal, minimal or choose the adequate one.

At times, there are simple choices, and at times, there are ones that are complicated. And sometimes, life throws impossible choices at you. I took a wrong decision of choosing biology in Class XI. By the time I realized my mistake, it was too late. The seats in commerce had already filled up. My pleas to the principal and the more empathetic vice-principal, P.K. Sehajwala, fell on deaf ears. My career was at stake here.

It was time to fix it. That was when my friend, Sunjay, intervened with a plan which he executed perfectly. The result? I joined the commerce stream which was important for me. Each time you solve a problem that seemed impossible, you become more fearless and confident; your risk-taking appetite goes up, and you are willing to push the envelope, which is exactly what you need to grow and run a business effectively.

Taking decisions, hence, becomes a habit, preparing you for the bigger ones. Parents and families who do not encourage or allow for an environment that endorses early decision-making, are committing an irreversible sin.

Sin 6: Not Providing Clarity to Your Children over Shareholding between Siblings and Cousins

A child tends to think that what his parents own is his alone. He might have a sibling, but he would never conceive that the business needs to be shared with his brother or sister and beyond. This assumption, of being a single owner, is a mighty challenge since it results in wrong expectations for the future. And even if this is resolved quickly, the next immediate challenge is to prepare him to share the business with cousins.

A bunch of cousins grow up in environments very different from each other. This is so because they are being raised by mothers coming from completely different backgrounds with their own methods, values and character. The same is then passed on to the children. Hence, there are two cousins who are very different in their approach towards the world, but they co-manage and co-share the business that they will eventually inherit.

The solution to both these challenges is fairly simple— clear communication with your children. This is one sin that parents and larger families need to be wary about. Telling your children about the reality of the inheritance and what the future would look like is essential. Not having absolute clarity in communication is a sin that you must avoid. You must tell them at the right time, and then it must be repeatedly reminded that, you and your brother(s) and cousin(s) are partners in this business. It is neither entirely theirs nor yours. You share it—whether you like it or not. In this family business, this is where you belong, and this is the part you own.

The louder, clearer and earlier the message is communicated, the better. Conflict arises only where there is misinformation, which creates dissonance between expectations and reality. A hairline difference between the two can trigger an avalanche of never-ending combat between brothers or cousins. And hence, with this communication, it is critical to set expectations right.

You need to tell them that each of them has a place in the larger scheme of things. Each one has ownership, but only over a designated percentage. A systematic ownership chart since the inception of the business can help understand how it started and how ownership is being transferred from one generation to the other.

For example, if two brothers started the business with a 60:40 shareholding:

Figure 5

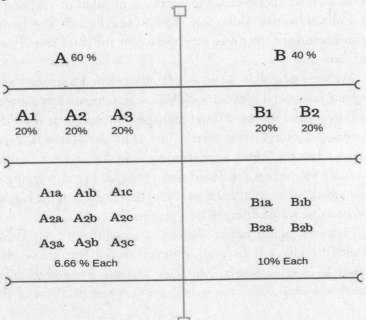

With each generation, the percentage that will be inherited by one owner can be reflected upon, and hence, it becomes clear that there are multiple owners with a different percentage of business ownership. What started in the first generation as a 60:40 partnership to create a business, becomes an equal partnership of 20 per cent each between five members of the second generation. The dawning of this reality makes them behave responsibly while managing the family and the business. The communication of the reality of ownership to the third generation will help them make more informed choices regarding their future.

This ownership chart also provides the option of taking only the ownership and not the management into consideration and doing something new altogether, whatever be the driving force. The example of Geep Flashlight Industries Ltd helps us understand this better. Geep, a leading brand of torches and batteries in India, was founded by M.R. Shervani, an astute businessman, who commanded great respect in the business community. His helping nature and social popularity made him gravitate towards politics. He became a member of Parliament of India. His two elder sons had joined him in the family business and the time was appropriate for the third son, Saeed, to follow suit.

We were neighbours and our families shared a strong bond, beyond just social pleasantries. We were informed that Saeed had decided to pursue a hotel management course at the Pusa Institute of Hotel Management in Delhi. The year was 1976! Times when traditions were strongly followed and not broken. It wasn't a deterrent for Saeed when tongues began wagging in Allahabad. Some went as far as saying that the son of the biggest industrialist was training to be a waiter.

However, in our house, the mood was different. My father would proudly tell us and whoever visited the house that 'Saeed is like his father, Mr Shervani. He has imbibed his entrepreneurial skills.' He would support the decision of the young lad and would confidently say, 'You wait and watch. He will be very successful.'

For the benefit of the reader, I would like to add here that I was curious to know exactly what had prompted Saeed to take such a step. He was candid about it and had two strong reasons for taking that step; there was no pretence. Having clarity of his ownership in the family business, Saeed could not see himself being part of its management. He was educated in a boarding school in Nainital and dreaded the thought of being back home, living in Allahabad and working with his elder brothers. He knew that the societal norm and family culture of 'elders always being right' and 'following the elder brothers' orders at any cost' would automatically reflect in the management of the family business too. He wanted to live differently. He wanted to be his 'own master'. I remember him joking about. '*Mujhe bhaiyon ki naukari nahin karni*' (I don't want to work for my brothers). Secondly, he had a strong sense of commitment towards the shareholders and other stakeholders of Geep Flashlight. He was very clear that, being the youngest, he would not be able to deliver what was expected from him within a public limited company.

Today, Saeed is a successful businessperson, a proud owner of the Shervani chain of hotels and the popular Mexican restaurant Rodeo in Connaught Place in Delhi.

The other advantage of having an ownership chart is to realize your own factual position within the family and the organization. If you notice, with every generation, the shareholding of one person keeps going down. So, in a way, the number of owners is increasing, but the percentage of ownership is decreasing and getting fragmented further. The ownership chart also acts as a support mechanism with the help of which one can explain why it is important to keep one's own vertical together.

Where there are more people, there is more politics; it is the nature of the world. In such a situation, the fragmentation of various owners needs to be brought together, and they need to act as one as far as decision-making is concerned. If you are united in the decision-making process, you automatically move in the right direction, and probably do not fall prey to the machinations of others.

In Baidyanath, we have five verticals operating in different geographical areas. I used the same wisdom to keep my vertical as one and experienced exponential results.

In case there are multiple businesses with a family, the significance of knowing your own shareholding becomes stronger. However, where families have multiple companies, what doesn't help is cross-holding, which is a definite area of future conflicts. It doesn't offer any positive results to anyone, but paves the way for obstructive practices. Hence, it is recommended that families clear up cross-holdings.

It is upon family elders and parents to safeguard their families and businesses from the psychological impact of children not being clear of their place in the family business. This sin can be avoided by considering the three-set theory talked about earlier whereby each family member is informed of their true position on the family business diagram.

Sin 7: Not Building a Good Character

Since the business is about a sharp mind, the mind must be fortified with moral courage. This courage comes from the foundation of a strong character.

Along with developing skills, promoting talent and cultivating values in children, parents must remember that it is a strong character that completes Brahmacharya. Only determined individuals fight their weaknesses to improve their character when they are adults. Most choose to rely on the way they were raised. Hence, instilling good character in the child becomes the responsibility of parents. Children learn from their parents; and it is often difficult to be an ideal example. But parents, remember, you are the child's most significant and powerful early influence. My grandmother, for some reason, would attribute breastfeeding as the start of character building of a child by a new parent.

What is character? Character defines who you are. It's the set of values and beliefs that determine your behaviour. It is your individual trait, the attitude that gives strength to your mind to act accordingly. So, even though you may have the skills, if you don't have a strong mind, it will be of no use. If skills are the arrows, you need a strong bow of character to hit the bullseye. Going back to the Mahabharata, the Kaurava and Pandava princes were raised in the same palace and were imparted similar skills. Yet, there were marked differences in character between them. Specifically, there is always a debate around the character of the oldest Kaurava prince—Duryodhana. It is necessary to compare the role of the mother, Kunti, who was focused on the development of the Pandava princes, with that of the upbringing of the Kauravas. Their father, King Dhritarashtra was born blind, and his wife Gandhari chose to remain blind towards her children. This made Duryodhana and Dushasana who they were.

While writing this book and interacting with the third generation entering Grihastha in their twenties, I was surprised to hear many of them having the same query: What if we missed out? Our parents might have overlooked this aspect. Can we, at this stage in life, strengthen our character? Yes, I suppose one can!

Parents may be the first and most significant influencers, but neighbours, friends, teachers, spouses, seniors, office colleagues, and many others also contribute towards and influence your character. Hence, there is no situation like missing out. I guess once you realize the need to change, half the battle is won. I recommend that you identify your weaknesses and flaws and improve upon them. And the battle is won.

Character is also directly linked to the right passion for money and achievements, which, in turn, are the ingredients for the making of a first-generation entrepreneur, or start-ups as we call them today. In my experience, three characteristics—self-esteem, confidence and integrity—are found in abundance in all successful entrepreneurs. These characteristics help them rise above basic needs as explained in Maslow's Hierarchy of Needs and motivate them to want more and move up the pyramid. Self-esteem makes you a confident individual, and confidence helps you to take decisions, and decisions taken with integrity result in the achievement of aspirations.

It is important for parents to instil the feeling that earning your own money is important. This comes naturally to a person with a strong character. Children from families of professionals are introduced to this idea very early in life. They have to focus on their studies because that will get them the right job to earn their living. In comparison, the children of business houses, at the same time, may get distracted with the luxuries of life or may take the family's success and money for granted. In the second and subsequent generations, children who don't learn that they need to make their own money are the ones who, further on in life, start to create conflicts with money in the family and the business. They harbour a feeling of being cheated and it makes them unhappy and jealous throughout their lives. The ones with a strong focus of earning their own money are the ones to lead the family business or diversify the group into other businesses.

My father was known for his strong character; it was, therefore, natural that he always gave preference to character—not just in the people he hired but also amongst friends and acquaintances. Once, I was travelling with him by car from Delhi to Dehradun (he used to make sure I accompanied him on his business trips). His very close friend, B.K. Goswami, an eminent IAS officer, was stationed in Meerut as Commissioner of Meerut Division at the time. He invited my father for a stopover. The plan was to have tea and move on. A sudden storm disrupted our travel plans and we had to spend the night at Goswami Uncle's place. That night, I clearly remember that the discussion over dinner centred on business families. I recall Billu Uncle as we call him sharing his experiences with my father. He said, 'All first-generation businessmen I know have a fire in their belly.' He continued, 'Ram, your father must also have had this intense desire to achieve. The second generation, like you, manages because you imbibe part of these great genes.' Then looking towards me, he said to my father, 'This generation has it all too easy. You must be careful. Don't let money spoil them. They have to work hard; they have to be strong-spirited and of a strong character. That is the only way they can take Baidyanath forward.'

He then elaborated on how two famous Indian brands of Ayurveda, Sukh Sancharak and Amritdhara, lost out because they lacked leadership. Billu Uncle is a revered bureaucrat. He is much admired and looked up to by all business houses who had the good fortune of interacting with him. Recently, I called him and reminded him of this old dinner conversation. I asked him what he thought were the traits that he found common in business families that have been successful. Pat came his reply, 'Ajay, if you want to know it in one word—it is *sanskar*.'

He got me thinking . . . I am not sure I can find an English equivalent to sanskar, which is a Hindi word used in Indian culture to denote someone's upbringing and thought process, ethics and moral behaviour. If we look at it differently, sanskar is a way of passing on lessons of good behaviour, knowledge and the wisdom of elders, which effectively translates into good character. Sanskar, in the Vedic context, is about enhancing the virtues in oneself and eliminating character flaws. For Indians, very simply put, it is the process of purifying oneself. To highlight the growing importance of sanskar, he mentioned that Amity University, a premium private educational institution with international footprints, is shortly opening up a university dedicated to innovation, technology and sanskar.

My father, a strong proponent of character, would frequently quote:

Sow a thought,
Reap an action.

Sow an action,
Reap a habit.

Sow a habit,
Reap character.

Sow character,
Reap a destiny.

When people say that destiny is in your hands, I guess they are urging one to introspect and enrich one's thoughts constantly. Why? Because actions are the consequence of directions given by the mind to the body and the mind decides from the available knowledge it holds. Therefore, a thought is based on the awareness and knowledge one has which converts into action. Any action that is performed repeatedly becomes a habit and habits of a person define their character which in turn moulds their destiny. In effect, Destination Destiny starts with knowledge that is available to a person and knowledge is only accumulated when there is a desire to do so.

Is character really that important? Lack of character translates into irresponsible behaviour. People who lack character are deficient in self-worth, which makes them behave in a disrespectful and arrogant manner. They can come across as egotistical and despotic, reasons strong enough for the family not to assign any role to them in business. Such traits are not conducive for healthy interpersonal relationships which are the backbone of a family business.

Sin 8: Not Being Exposed to Higher Education

Education, in the simplest form, is training your mind to think and communicate in a structured way. Going further, general education these days helps to elevate one from poverty. It is higher education that prepares students to face the challenges of a more complex nature—be it management, medicine, politics or family business.

If we relook at the sequence of our sins in Brahmacharya, first comes skill, followed by gaining wisdom by going out of one's comfort zone, and backed by strong character. The icing on the cake is the knowledge gained through higher education. This knowledge makes you aware of what exists and gives you more options to choose from. It allows you to pursue a career of your choice and makes you financially self-sufficient. It's what defines your destiny.

You will find people making claims such as, 'It's only the price that matters for selling a product, nothing else'. Someone who has studied business will never make such a statement. These are random statements made by folks who are not exposed to higher education and hence, may not be aware of the 4Ps of marketing—product, price, place and promotion, or perhaps they may know of these concepts, but do not know how to put them to use. This is just a rudimentary example showcasing the difference between someone who has not been exposed to higher education as compared to someone who has been made complete by virtue of such knowledge gain. Higher education teaches you how to apply the knowledge that it imparts. It teaches you to see situations from different perspectives, and analyse every situation to arrive at decisions for reaching one's desired goals.

Today, children need to look at specific courses for specialization in various fields while pursuing higher education to further strengthen the family business as a suitable successor. In mid-level family businesses, there is a common misconception that you have to be 'street-smart' to be able to 'handle' people (labourers, labour union leaders, inspectors, bureaucrats, etc.). Being street-smart does give you an immediate dedicated manager but not a successor suited for your business. Parents may feel that starting early will help the continuity of the business, but the successor might actually turn out to be a square peg in a round hole. On the other hand, pursuing a higher education can help them to discover themselves and know exactly what they want to do. For the ones who choose to continue the business, higher education exposes them to concepts and practical realities such as investments, capital decisions, finance, strategy, management, mergers and acquisitions, leadership, negotiations—all of which are far more relevant for a successor–owner.

The world is changing at a pace that is faster than ever before, and so is technology, which affects every aspect of life. Education at a higher level is about becoming more specialized and focused on providing solutions. From engineering to medicine, psychology to information technology, hospitality to healthcare, from managing shares and funds to managing family businesses, whatever stream of specialization one takes up, the orientation is towards looking for answers, unravelling theories and finding solutions. It makes the student diligent and a problem-solver, characteristics that are prerequisites to take the family along in the family business.

In my case, my early entry into the business was an experiment by the elders of the family to enrol me into the 'university of experience'. However, mid-Grihastha, I felt the need for higher education—the 'university of knowledge' to gain insights related to business to manage the growing organization. Business owners often say, 'Why waste so much time and money when I can put my child straight into business? After all, it is practical experience which is the end-all of running a successful business and theory is all on paper.' Higher education is not something you pursue to pass time, or a sabbatical to enjoy travel. It is, in fact, an investment. Sometimes, even a single year of specialized education can give more insights, exposure and add growth than the initial five years of working in the family business. Hence, while I am a propagator of formal higher education, I do not discount the importance of early experience in family business.

A lot of children from business families these days are in a dilemma about whether to pursue higher education immediately after graduation or after gaining experience in the family business. 'When is the right time to pursue a higher education?' is the eternal question.

'Should I go for it immediately after my graduation?'

'Should I work in the business for a couple of years so that I can relate to what they are teaching?' (Most MBA programmes require a minimum of two years' work experience.) There are other pressures and reasons for children from business families to pursue higher education like, 'I have a deadline to get married, so I have to complete my education before that'; 'I need to get out of the family environment, so I need to study'; or 'Just because my elder cousins have studied abroad, I have to follow suit'. Are these the right reasons for pursuing a higher education? Each child is unique and parents need to be sensitive about their expectations from their children, as undue pressure does not yield satisfactory results.

The closest example I can share is of my own son. He went to the University of Illinois Urbana-Champaign, USA, for his undergraduate studies in mechanical engineering. He was a science student and had never studied business in school. After graduation, he was eager to work in the family business in order to be exposed to the practical aspects of what business is and also to experience the family business environment. While working for the family business, he found his calling and told me, 'Dad, now I am more aware of the shortcomings in my own knowledge and would want to fill this void by pursuing higher education.' In his case, it was a post-graduation in business. He is currently pursuing his MBA from London Business School in London.

Higher education is not a natural progression in an individual's educational journey in the Brahmacharya Ashram. It is a conscious and voluntary step towards self-evolution to face the challenges of the world and seek knowledge. It is unique to each individual and their state of mind. Hence, plotting everyone against a standard graph would be unfair.

Sin 9: Not Spending Time with Spouse and Children

I have experienced a proud first generation boasting how they barely have time for their families as they are engrossed in business. It is obvious that they are doing so for their spouse and children, providing them with comforts and luxury. They are proud that they will be handing over a strong money-making machinery to their children, but it is a poor justification for not giving time to their families.

The family, in such cases, suffers. If you are worried about the continuity and growth of your business and don't just want your kids to merely inherit it—there is no other way than spending time with your spouse and family to understand who they are and who they are becoming in the course of time. You have to observe your children and learn what they are good at and, perhaps, guide them and help them cope with mental challenges. Moral values like respect for all, honesty towards work and importance of family are cultivated by good parenting and not by forcing it upon them.

And surprisingly, such ignorance is not a rare occurrence. While I do not deny that it doesn't happen in subsequent generations, first-generation cases are relatively higher—as much as seven out of ten. Good parenting in terms of a family business is instilling love for the family and respect for the business.

A first-generation business must be inherited by the second generation for it to become a family business. The biggest reason why the creator of the business sells off his business is because there is no competent successor available in the second generation. Spending time with the spouse and children helps parents collectively groom a successor to pass on a created business, and the family wealth. For the second generation, spending time with the spouse and children helps focus on eliminating conflicts arising out of the opinions of multiple members in a growing family, thus ensuring continuity. The third generation, as parents, are aware that very few businesses survive through the third generation. Therefore, they groom their children to respect the wealth created by their elders. The sole focus becomes safeguarding family wealth and name by feeling obligated about the inheritance.

I still remember when my first child was born, my wife was aware of my schedules and travel routine. She was aware that even though I was a family man, I was equally, if not more, passionately involved in my business at the time. So, she, in her own characteristic way, reminded me, 'Ajay, we both have our individual childhood memories that are lovely. Let's not deprive Rishi of it. Let's create memories for him to remember and cherish.' I have always been aware of the two sets—set A (family) and set B (business)—but the reminder made me consciously maintain a fine balance between them since that day.

An example that I'd like to share here is of a close friend who married an educated young girl from a family of professionals. While her son was growing up, she was exposed to the challenges of a family business and would mention in conversations that she would prefer the child to have a proper degree and become a professional. She felt a business had its insecurities and risks, and continuity could not be guaranteed. A well-paying professional job was exactly the opposite. Since my friend remained busy with his family business, his wife raised the child with her own set of values and ideas. When he grew up, the son himself shunned the family business and pursued law. This disconnect led to a bitter conflict between the couple. Having a collective goal could have avoided this crisis.

You have to understand that your life partner is a stakeholder in the family business too; both of you are equal participants in raising the heir. The child's values are an assimilation of both the parents' thoughts and beliefs, but the spouse is the one who is around the child in the formative years. Hence, you have to communicate in an appropriate way—just the way you would do with a stakeholder. Your aspirations for your children must arrive at a common point with your spouse since they might come from a different background and have different beliefs. You need to invest time in having clear communication about the future role of the child within the family and the business.

A study of family businesses from the perspective of this sin reveals some interesting facts. People who successfully run their family business owe it to the great connect they share with their parents, to the family values that were handed down to them by their elders and also to the time they continuously spent and continue to do so with their spouses and children. To sum it up, there are nine must-dos for good parenting or grandparenting if we desire to have successful leaders for the family business.

It is because of these virtues inculcated in children that family businesses become successful.

+ Instilling respect for the family business
+ Building a sense of security for each individual
+ Inculcating family values
+ Providing advice on how to cope with challenges
+ Building confidence
+ Working towards facilitating emotional well-being
+ Ensuring positive behaviour
+ Working towards nipping behavioural problems in the bud
+ Ensuring clear, open, constructive and two-way communication

Grihastha T2:
Figure 6

SECOND STAGE

STAGE	ASHRAM	4 Ts	GOAL
I	Brahmacharya	Training	Knowledge
II	Grihastha	Transaction	Wealth
III	Vanaprastha	Transition	Fame
IV	Sanyas	Turn-in	Relinquishment

My transition to Grihastha from Brahmacharya was not clearly demarcated. A twist of fate got me back to my hometown Allahabad to complete my graduation at Allahabad University. It is also known as the Oxford of the East owing to its meritorious and historical past of being one of the oldest modern universities of India. Allahabad, for all its grandeur, is a laidback town with two strong interests: politics and literature. No wonder it gave the country seven prime ministers. It was also home to authors like Munshi Premchand, Mahadevi Verma, Harivansh Rai Bachchan and Firaq Gorakhpuri, to name a few.

The energy and environment of the town were not enticing enough for the children of business families. And hence, we were on a quest to find out what would attract us. Be it the only restaurant–El-Chico, or the newly-mushroomed video parlours, a dominating trend of that era; everyone had found something or the other to suit themselves. But I could barely feel excited about those video parlours. They were just not real enough, and I started spending more time at our plant located in the Naini industrial area, on the outskirts of Allahabad.

On seeing that my visits to the plant were more frequent than usual, Colonel Uncle, our general manager, and his wife, Krishna Aunty, who resided within the factory premises, began inviting me to their house. Colonel S.P. Sharma (Retd.) was earlier posted at the Allahabad Fort with the army and had met my father at a social event. One thing led to another and he joined our company as general manager. The lunch and evening tea sessions at Uncle's house were initially spent over conversations about forgotten stories from my childhood. But soon enough, the conversation started moving towards current happenings within the plant and in the business.

The time I spent with the couple was so stimulating that I started skipping classes and was there at the plant and office for hours together. I had no formal business training then. Today, when I look back, I realize that Uncle and Aunty were my first business teachers. They were the ones who taught me practical skills at our biggest manufacturing plant in India.

I cannot particularly pinpoint if it was my interest which was encouraged by my father, but I was naturally absorbed by our business. I felt like a fish taking to water. Much later, my uncle told me that he and my father had decided to make me the experiment child by not sending me for higher studies and exposing me to the business early. That explains why my father declined to send me to the US for my undergraduation studies. At the time, I would wonder that, while he had himself enrolled in Cornell University in the US and later went to England for his chemical engineering, why hadn't he encouraged me to study overseas? Many answers come much later on in life, I guess!

Grihastha is the transaction phase. It is where you enter the business and take responsibility. It is here where you marry and start a family. It is here that you are in control and you have to own your choices. In Brahmacharya, it was your parents and elders who were taking the decisions for you. The grooming phase is now officially over and it is time to act and deliver. Your parents, perhaps, made the right choices for you, during the Brahmacharya Ashram. They might make the right ones for Grihastha too. But you are the owner of Grihastha and the ownership of choices is yours and the outcome of those choices is yours too. You have to consciously be aware of not committing the following sins.

Sin 10: Not Identifying Your Passion and Pursuing It

As a child, I was very careful with money. During our holidays, my father would personally give us daily pocket money and would keep tabs on our spending. Invariably, after every holiday, I would return home with unspent money. It is not that I didn't enjoy spending during the holidays like my siblings and cousins. But at the same time, spending judiciously on what I needed rather than what I wanted was intrinsic. My parents noticed my attitude towards money over the years and saw a finance guy in me. Hence, before I joined the business, I was encouraged to do chartered accountancy. I appeared for my first paper and, while awaiting my results, started visiting a renowned chartered accountant in the city to get a sense of the job. I went there for five days and decided not to show up after that. My father was informed of my act of defiance and he questioned me about it. I simply answered, 'It's boring. I need more creativity and I need to do something that I am passionate about.'

Later, I became an out-and-out marketing guy. I enjoyed travelling and being out in the field. So, many-a-time, your traits, actions and characteristics are misread by your parents and mentors. At times, your passion stays latent. Your parents may claim to know you. But you are more than what meets the eye. Also, it usually happens that parents try to fulfil their own dreams and passions through you. Then who do you think is the person who really knows you? It's you. The importance of Brahmacharya, the first stage of life, is to help you identify your passion. Once you have explored and tried multiple things in life during the Brahmacharya phase or early Grihastha, you will have a clear understanding of what you enjoy and what you don't. This helps one identify their passion.

And remember, your passion can also simply be making money, which is absolutely fair. In that case, whatever you are doing that brings in revenue can become your passion and you can adapt to that. The crux of the matter is to succeed. Because a successful person will never be a burden on their family or the family business. In fact, they have the resources to give, forgive and forgo.

Every single day that I went to the CA firm, I wanted to run back to the factory and spend time at the plant to work on the small assignments that I had undertaken. I kept thinking about them when I sat at my desk. This made me realize what I was really passionate about and I decided to follow it.

My father, who observed my visits to the plant and the small contributions I made towards the management of the business, decided that it was time for me to formally enter the business. I readily agreed since I was sure that it was what I wanted to do; where my interests lay.

This reminds me of the internationally acclaimed fashion designer, Gaurav Gupta, who belongs to the third generation in a business family. Expectations that he would take the family iron and steel business forward were natural. While still in his teens, he expressed his desire to pursue fashion designing.

Gaurav said, 'Luckily, my father was open-minded and realized that I was very focused as a teenager and knew what I wanted to do.' Despite the views and pressures of the larger joint family to the contrary, his father struck a deal with Gaurav. He said, 'If you get admission in a top fashion school, you can pursue your passion.' This is a methodology parents often adopt to check just how serious their children are. Gaurav got through in NIFT, Delhi, and later studied at Central Saint Martins in London. The rest is history! A star was born!

How does one identify a passion? Gaurav advises the young thus, 'It should not come from a sense of rebellion but a sense of purpose.' He strongly advocates that the dream one wants to pursue should be commercially viable.

A role model for millions who want to follow their heart's desire, Gaurav has some advice for parents whose children want to move away from the family business and do their own thing. 'Give them a timeline for success, say, five to seven years. That is enough for anyone to convert their passion into success.'

The identification of a passion is important. While it needs to be pursued to achieve commercial success, rebellion should not be the driving force behind wanting to do something different, just to move away from the family business. For a parent, it's a bitter pill to swallow that the child does not want to continue the family business; they take it as a judgemental move. Hence, they don't address the issue of the child wanting to pursue something new. But let's not forget that the family business too was started by someone in the family who did something different from what the earlier generation was doing. Learning about the true passion of your child will create new businesses. It will also encourage youngsters to diversify or branch out, a healthy requirement in expanding families.

Sin 11: Delaying Early Division

Inducting someone from a family into a business is tricky; you cannot just step in. There are existing stakeholders and, more importantly, there are existing owners. Is there space for them, are they required to play a role, are internal questions that need answers.

While studying the successful leading Marwari and Gujarati business communities of India, I noticed a recurring induction pattern. As soon as the children reach Grihastha, they are either handed over independent management or ownership of the existing business or given capital to start afresh. They ensure that the next generation's start is in a clean environment which is theirs to build and grow and the ownership is theirs. Ownership infuses a sense of commitment to succeed, it generates the passion and enthusiasm of a start-up entrepreneur. By executing an early division, the family becomes a group of diversified new businesses which also translates into growth of the existing business. Most importantly, it encourages healthy inter-family support and pushes each young member to give their best. Personally, I am a great propagator of this ethic since it ensures early division of ownership, management, or preferably ownership and management and longevity of families. The goodwill such families create helps all members and their respective new or old businesses. The brand value of one brand strengthens the others and it builds on.

To understand our case, let's step back a bit and look at the history of Baidyanath. My grandfather, along with his younger brother, founded the company in 1917. He had six sons. The eldest took an early exit to follow his passion of publishing a newspaper and pursuing politics.

My grandfather was a visionary, a disciplinarian and a strong administrator. It was not just the business, but the family too revolved around him. He was committed to anything and everything he touched, and it belonged to him. He was a towering personality. When his eldest son decided to contest for assembly elections in our home state of Rajasthan, the opponent—who was the maharaja of the principality—decided to withdraw from the election. Such was my grandfather's charisma!

He passed away early, while still executing his duties of Vanaprastha, in 1963. We were left with an undivided business, held by a family that was bound together with strong family values. Siblings and cousins (the sons of my grandfather's brother) developed a working understanding of the business. It was then divided into five verticals, each having individual manufacturing capacities and operating in well-defined geographical markets for a regional push. The objective was to maximize reach by dividing India into five regions or zones and taking advantage of the behaviour and spending patterns of regional consumers. On the family front, it gave my uncles and my father the freedom to operate independently while sharing the ownership of the overall brand. The model was of joint ownership of business with family members being utilized in management.

I was born in the same year that my grandfather passed away. I was a toddler when this arrangement took place. I was under the tutelage of my grandmother who would tell me all about the business that her husband had founded and the strengths of the family. She was a storehouse of information and had an iron will, but was also very compassionate. On several evenings, while we had atta laddoos and mathri-achaar (a flaky savoury biscuit accompanied by pickle), she would impart her wisdom to her grandchildren. I remember that while everyone else would run away to play after snacking to their heart's content, she would hold me back and tell me stories of past, present and possible future events. Our sessions continued for a long time. Even when I used to visit home for the holidays while I was studying at Mayo, we would resume our evening conversations from where we had left off earlier.

She was well-informed of the current affairs and would express unhappiness at some events taking place in the country since she saw them as signals of things to come. She would fear the impact of those events on her own family—India and Pakistan were at war in 1971, Bangladesh was being created and Himachal Pradesh had been carved out of Punjab. These divisions, she felt, would encourage similar thoughts within the family.

Later, Emergency was imposed; all schemes related to family planning reforms in India failed; the Janata Dal won, putting Congress out of power for the first time since Independence; the Congress split; there was a takeover bid by Swaraj Paul for two of north India's biggest businesses of that time—Escorts and DCM. While the country was facing chaos, there was turmoil playing out in our family too! The Calcutta vertical had operations and management issues. Units became independent, almost operating as standalone companies with inter-unit discipline at the minimum that was ever seen in business. Moreover, by the early 1980s, the third generation that I belong to was gearing up to enter business, while the second was now dealing with the passing away of the older uncle who had been managing the flagship vertical in Patna.

As a typical grandmother, she was worried about her grandchildren in the third generation and, similarly, about the business that her husband and his younger brother had created. She could see the cracks appearing in the Birla family, which was considered the role model for any business family, especially those hailing from Rajasthan. And, of course, there was the emergence of the Ambani family with their popular venture in the textile industry—Vimal, which was giving well-established family businesses a run for their money. She was aware of competition coming up in the ayurvedic industry too, and apprised us of our role in ensuring that the most trusted ayurvedic brand always retained its leadership position.

Business families were faced with the question of plenty—in terms of the number of members—putting pressure on the income. Our family was not insulated from this phenomenon. While two verticals were being managed by younger uncles who had entered Grihastha recently, the other three were being managed by my Tau ji (my father's elder brother), my father and my Chacha ji (my father's younger brother). All three had two grown-up sons each, who were ready to embark on their individual Grihastha journeys.

The three elders of the family came up with a strategy that the vertical they had inherited would be managed and operated by one of the sons only. The other son would be given the important responsibility of diversifying the family business since that was the mantra of the era! My father had recently seen the success of his neighbour's youngest son (as mentioned earlier) and how he had diversified into a separate business. My father knew that this was the only way to go forward. Tau ji chose a backward vertical-integration approach and started a new factory for manufacturing containers and other packaging materials. Chacha ji took the local advantage in Jhansi and decided to enter the mining business. My father chose to enter the FMCG business of branded atta in Delhi.

Things were changing very rapidly. Business families that were caught napping were faced with huge challenges. At Baidyanath, the two younger uncles from the second generation that was in command, took stock of the situation. Asiad '82 had introduced colour televisions pan-India, giving rise to the opportunity of advertising nationally and taking brands to the next level. My youngest uncle, stationed in Calcutta, who was back after doing his MBA from Fairleigh Dickinson University in the US, was introducing modern practices in our business. The other, with a degree from BITS Pilani, was patronizing Ayurveda with modern inputs. They both saw an opportunity in the success of *Ramayan*, the classic serial telecast on TV and its impact on the population of India. They witnessed the zeal with which the common populace was happy to drop everything they were doing to watch Ram take on Ravana on TV. Both saw India transforming from regional to national and realized that our regional advantages would diminish eventually. It was time for Baidyanath to sponsor *Ramayan* and go national. They took one step in the right direction. Competition was also on the rise. Continuity of the business was the priority for the family, and they devised new learnings to improve inter-unit coordination to project a singular brand image while safeguarding the ownership structure within the family. While their choices were justified, it must still be highlighted that it was nowhere close to a true division or a consolidation. Management was still at five locations and no business activity like manufacturing, marketing or purchase was under one roof. Fortunately, though, the family had managed to evolve a working structure unique to the organization.

All families are not fortunate to implement a cohesive structure; instead, to provide work for every member, some families allocate each child to one department that they are to manage, like marketing, finance, purchase, manufacturing, etc. You may assume that they will behave like managers when, in effect, they are owners with self-assigned authority. Hence, conflicts are inevitable. Dividing management of departments of one company and assuming that the division has been taken care of, is living in a fool's paradise. In fact, it is the fastest route to confirm and execute the curse. In our case, the five verticals operated as strategic business units, which did not face such a situation but each was thinking differently; each had their own vision for the future of the brand. Dividing early in the true sense or choosing a successor to manage on behalf of the family is a better solution. It instils an important first-generation trait of passion for succeeding in the business and provides income for other shareholders of the business.

'Build an empire together while working as one force.'

Well, empires are not built by a single person. At the same time, empires are not built to be divided. They are built to benefit everyone.

'A chariot pulled by four horses moves faster than one drawn by a single horse.'

True, if they are tied together under a charter and a direction is maintained. Imagine if two horses run in one direction and the other two in another, the chariot will be broken into two pieces in no time.

Families that believe in such philosophies are conditioned to think like this because of the same agrarian mindset which believes that more hands will help grow more food. *This is a fallacy of ownership.* In a family with a diverse set of skills, family members think it is appropriate to amalgamate all and make it one. While this may sound theoretically perfect, it is not the right way as things can go horribly wrong.

Philosophically speaking, we come alone into the world and depart alone. I am not cynical, hear me out. Our challenges are our own, and so are our skills and merits. We go through training and development for our own self, so then, why not do the business ourselves? In our journey of life, we find advisers, gurus and supporters. While they might play a pivotal role in shaping us or our business, we do not share ownership with them.

Having multiple owners for the same business is fatal as you may create two or more competitors. Hence, the elders of the family should push for a sensible division of wealth. To understand this further, let us consider the happenings at the Bajaj household.

Bajaj Auto was in the business of scooters since the mid-1940s. Market conditions must have given them the opportunity to start a division for financing scooters and three-wheelers, which grew exponentially. When the time came for Grihastha for the next generation, the family made two separate non-competing businesses out of it—one being the manufacturing and selling of scooters and the other being finance. A move by the father, Rahul Bajaj, to unlock shareholder value, simultaneously gave an opportunity to the next generation to head two different non-competing businesses. If we refer to the three-set theory, this seems like a win, win and win situation for all the three sets—set A (family), set B (business) and set C (shareholders). The essence of maintaining non-competing businesses is to keep the family together and avoid conflict.

There can be numerous possibilities of division. Consider a case where there is a formidable flagship business of the family and it appears to be indivisible—like that of Ranbaxy—a successful first-generation enterprise. The father had three sons and it is public knowledge that the forerunner, Ranbaxy, went to the eldest. Montari Industries Limited went to his second son along with some other assets. Analjit Singh, his youngest, got Max, along with some assets and capital. This available capital could have been the impetus for him to build an empire in Max Hospitals. All divisions are not amicable. But who has seen the future? The third generation at Ranbaxy sold the company and followed in their uncle's footsteps by starting Fortis Hospitals, a competing business.

One has to realize the need to divide and then act on it. You will see that there are endless possibilities. But they must be exerted and implemented. Dividing doesn't mean breaking down and making an existing business less productive. Even though it seems counterintuitive to divide in order to keep the family together, it is the ones who don't divide the business that end up dividing the families. Early or timely division in each generation can keep creating first-generation families, and hence prevent the trap of being the third generation and, eventually, turning into Mahesh, the destroyer.

A situation may also arise for the elders when one sibling is not as competent as the other. The easy way out, then, is for families to make them piggyback on the successful sibling. Let me take you back to the wisdom of the Marwari community. They are quick to make sure that the incompetent one and his family are taken care of by assets and rental arrangements. Hence, it is not mandatory that after division, a new business must arise. The objective is that the family must survive comfortably and with dignity.

Early division ensures successful businesses and a strong family name. A virtue which should be a culture in all family businesses.

Sin 12: Trying to Fit into Someone Else's Shoes

Now let's assume that early division goes through and you are given charge of the family business or that you enter the family business being managed solely by your father. When you enter the transaction stage (Grihastha Ashram) and start learning the ropes to ultimately lead the business, there is immense pressure to fill the shoes of the predecessor.

To fill someone's shoes is to take over the position and responsibilities of that person. While you have entered or taken over the business, there will be people who will expect you to 'fit' into those shoes. This is exactly what you should not succumb to. Don't try to fit into the shoes of the predecessor, because they are his shoes and you are not him. Everyone has an individual style, and, with changes in time and authority, the shoes must change too.

When I entered the business, there were expectations that I would not just operate but even behave like my father. Our company employees, managers, customers and stakeholders expected the same treatment from me, which can be narrowed down to as much as of my way of greeting people. I concluded that my father was highly revered—he was a demi-god of sorts—and my job of making my own mark had just become harder.

It would have been easier to ape him. But I did not succumb under pressure. I stood for myself, I built my own leadership.

Till those expectations persist, the mercury says you have not made your mark. Success evades you. Remember, people follow successful people. Then there are stakeholders like suppliers and dealers who might not like you trying to do things differently and might even complain or pass comments—directly or indirectly. These are pressures to make you fit the shoe and not fill one.

'You are so much like your father.' They would tell me so that I followed my father's style. This would, obviously, keep employees in their existing comfort zones and they would not have to change with the advent of the new generation. They were insecure. They were scared of change as there were chances of them losing the power and position they had been enjoying so far. Thus, you must not give in to their expectations and not try to replicate the ways of the predecessor. While it is important to maintain the core ethics of the business, the values of the organization and the credibility of the brand, it is not necessary to do so exactly in the way the predecessor did. Trying to do so might actually put a halt to the continuity of the business.

The objective is to go from point A to point B. The number of steps you may have to take can vary, the mode of travel can be different; you may need a different set of managers to accompany you on this journey and you can also choose an alternate route to reach your destination. The old guards, who know they cannot be a part of this journey with you, see their relevance decreasing. They are the ones who want you to 'fit' into the shoe. In effect, they want you to follow the same ways and have the same opinions about them as the predecessor. They are, in fact, looking at their own survival while you have taken on the job of making the business survive and thrive.

The first generation has no baggage of 'This is how it is done'. It is the second that has to hear statements from the management like, 'This is how we do it', or 'This is the company way'. Some stronger ones are 'Your father has put this system in place' or 'It's your father's success formula', putting the second generation in a quandary. If one changes it, it's viewed as a form of disrespect to the first generation's ways, or defiance towards the father. At times, it can be communicated mischievously to the family. These are all methods of making the second generation 'fit' into the shoe. Remember, you are Vishnu, so one has to take a leaf out of His management style.

When you step up to manage the business, you don't automatically become the leader of the team. You have to inspire and engage the team; show them the bigger picture and take everyone along. You have to make them understand the importance of moving from a nimble quick-response first-generation management style to a more formal, structured organization. Change should be reasoned with before being executed, or else managers will go downhill.

While your Brahmacharya has gone right and you have been chosen rightly to be a successor or the chosen successor to lead and manage the business, you must forge your own path and prove yourself to earn respect and lead from the front. You might very well draw learnings and use insights from the previous generation, but you need not copy. The third generation faces other challenges too—they have to get the employees to stay loyal to the organization beyond their own self-interest. Change should benefit all, create a win-win situation, or else, managers will set you up for failure. Taking on the role with the preconceived thought that all old and existing teams of managers are not relevant is a sin of caution that you must not commit. It is cited as one of the top external reasons why the third generation does not succeed.

A message for the generation that is going through Vanaprastha is that while handing over to the successor, give freedom for implementation. Continuity is now the next generation's responsibility, and they must take care of it in the way they can manage and sustain it right. It is your responsibility to teach and guide them with advice on all that helped you, but you should let them become the entrepreneurs they are meant to be.

Leaders are self-aware and comfortable in their own shoes and thus have the ability to stand out, take risks, stay self-motivated and focus on their people to realize their vision.

Sin 13: Following the 'If It Ain't Broke, Don't Fix It' Principle

At Baidyanath, we've always had a very elaborate set-up to manufacture, pack and dispatch medicines. In Ayurveda, raw materials undergo a tedious and labour-intensive process of cleaning, sorting, detoxifying and neutralizing. This, again, is reprocessed for the manufacture of medicines. The organization takes pride in its manufacturing practices, something that prompted three Indian prime ministers to visit our plant in Naini—Jawaharlal Nehru, Lal Bahadur Shastri and Indira Gandhi. No mean feat, that!

My time at Mayo had exposed me to Indian royalty—they are a proud lot, who value their legacy and appreciate the past. They are proud of their ancestors' accomplishments and their own commitment towards their people. Most possess constructive pride, but pride has a destructive side too. It makes one rigid, arrogant and fills one up with a boastful self-view. However, I witnessed that the same royalty no longer discussed the withdrawal of the privy purse. Instead, they were changing with the times; converting their palaces and forts into hotels to live with dignity. Change was taking place in the most rigid of cultures. I am a big fan of Bob Dylan and believed in him when he sang the popular song, 'The times, they are a-changin'.

Respecting our pride and legacy at Baidyanath, when I joined the business, I was quick to spot that the era of manufacturing that had been ruling the roost was moving to one of manufacturing and distribution. And the one who could manufacture and deliver safely and on time was the winner. There was a paradigm shift.

Plastic had not invaded the packaging scene yet at the time. All our medicines were packed in glass bottles or tin containers. These would then be packed in jute sacks or cane baskets, but primarily in wooden crates, for onward dispatches. We had logs of wood delivered to the plant. These logs were cut into thin planks by gigantic machines to create crates of wood. To prevent breakage of glass bottles, due protection was provided by meticulously cushioning each glass bottle in a layer of hay before being packed into wooden crates. The complete process was done in-house. Today's globalized world would be a bit shocked, but those were the times of being self-sufficient.

I had been to an innovative show at Pragati Maidan in New Delhi which was becoming a great venue for trade fairs and conventions. It is here that I got the idea of introducing corrugated paper boxes for packing—a modern concept—for hassle-free outward movement and supply. They could replace wooden crates, saving the company considerable time and money. I brought the idea to the company but it was an enormous task to make a convincing argument given that trade unions back then were strong and had a tendency to oppose any change suggested by the management. These tactics would keep them relevant in the eyes of the worker. Some of the senior managers too were not in favour of it. However, my father and the general manager were convinced and decided to go ahead with it. We grew by 100 per cent in two years because of this decision. While it was the achievement of my father and his team, the stakeholders showered me with accolades for this achievement.

'If it ain't broke, don't fix it.' While Bert Lance made the statement popular, he said it in the context of the government. Somehow, this phrase crept into business, but as wise as it might sound, I strongly feel that it doesn't apply here. Business is about change. What might not be obviously broken, might be obsolete and hence, must be upgraded. Change is a must.

You need to keep reviewing systems, processes, norms and rules, and you need to keep changing them since they might have become irrelevant with time. People resist change. It is in their nature. But as clichéd as it may sound, change is the only constant in the world, and for a business, it is imperative to embrace it.

This brings me to the most famous and often-discussed case study—that of Kodak and Fujifilm—whose businesses, though similar in many ways, went in two opposite directions. The world had captured and framed the 'Kodak moment', which seems to have gone away forever, while Fujifilm not only survived but scaled newer heights.

The obsession with storing memories made film sales a booming business, with Kodak and Fujifilm being the leaders who controlled a majority of market sales. With the start of the digital era, markets began shrinking slowly and suddenly plummeted to a disastrous low. Change was in the air.

The digital era, which took over in the 1990s, prompted consumers to purchase the all-new digital cameras. Witnessing the digital onslaught, in 2006, the CEO of Kodak, Antonio Perez, called digital cameras a 'crappy business'; when we recall it today, it indicates a refusal of sorts. At the same time, Fujifilm accepted reality and overcame the crisis through innovation and external growth. They saw the potential of existing technologies within the company as those with future growth potential in pharmaceuticals and cosmetics. Through a massive diversification drive, they rode the wave. Kodak, meanwhile, could not adapt to the rapidly growing digital world.

Was it that Kodak suffered from myopia and did not see the digital camera coming? Or did complacency get the better of them? Did the senior management not accept the inevitable even though they were aware of the incoming digital tsunami? The pride of being the leader had probably made the senior management at Kodak bask in destructive pride. Kodak broke apart for the same reason that Fujifilm rebuilt its brand: the will to change. Living with humble dignity makes one survive but rigid pride can be destructive.

This is where you need to open your third eye, the eye of wisdom. Your two eyes help you see what is apparent and obvious. But it is only your third eye which helps you to see what's beyond. Fujifilm's management strongly believed that a peak always conceals a treacherous valley. The opening of their third eye of wisdom helped the company overcome the crisis.

It is not all about data and what is apparent. It is about gathering knowledge about the possible future, instead of condemning it; it is about the ability to adapt and change as per the situation. And if you can manage this change, you can break the curse. To not be a victim of the sin, keep asking yourself in every situation—is this relevant? Even Darwin's theory suggests that it's not the strongest or the smartest species that survive. It's the one which adapts and changes. It is scientific.

The early achievement that I had by breaking the conception of 'If it ain't broke, don't fix it', opened the gates for people to take me rather seriously. This helped me to manage manpower better. I hired better-skilled supervisors and, most importantly, the attitude of the labour unions towards me became soft since they could probably feel the 'winds of change'—this is another of my favourite songs, which talks about awakening society through change, sung by the Scorpions. I could build a robust sales team which could deliver easy implementation of my newer marketing concepts. The company went on to host the first-ever dealers conference at the famous El-Chico restaurant. Such early successes and achievements in business help you to position yourself strongly in the existing set-up, and you are likely to be accepted more easily within the organization, while you are in the initial leg of your journey of Grihastha.

Sin 14: Burning Yourself and Not Lighting Up

'Life is a celebration.'

This is something I understood in the early years of my Grihastha. I had realized my passion; I was achieving something or the other every day and business was ever-demanding. However, between work and studies, I decided to follow what I had learnt at Mayo—keep a balance and participate in other activities that make you happy. Giving oneself a break from work is a widely understood fact and is made popular by the proverb, 'All work and no play makes Jack a dull boy'. As soon as this realization dawned upon me, I started looking for some form of recreation. It presented itself in the form of a squash court.

Allahabad had a huge settlement of people from the army and the air force. Their lives were largely limited to the cantonment and they hardly interacted with civilians, as we were referred to. I got to know that the army cantonment very close to our house had a squash court and I went on a quest to get access to it. After great difficulty, I was finally able to access it, which created an opening for me to mingle with the army crowd, besides enjoying a couple of games of squash with them. I started being invited to their ballroom parties and other social events. Visiting the cantonments made me nostalgic as it reminded me of the discipline and etiquette we followed at Mayo. I was heavily influenced by the humility the army men displayed. Despite having all the power in the world, I could never see arrogance in a single officer. This helped me to build my own character. So much so that at a point in life, I considered joining the Territorial Army.

My new friends from the army were like-minded. They were hard-working, humorous and knew how to celebrate life while they were constantly preparing themselves for war. This learning was phenomenal and that is how I could find a balance in my life, and this reflected well in my work.

My father was a member of the Army Golf Club and, on seeing my routine, he took out his golf set and asked me to try my hand at golf. I was elated and felt special since none of us (children) were ever allowed to touch his things (even a pen was out of bounds), leave aside using them. I picked up the golf set and went straight to my neighbour and childhood friend, Kaju. I knew he was interested in golf. And we were off to the greens. K.N. Singh, former chief justice of India, an ardent golfer, was playing on the course. He was a judge in Allahabad High Court during those days. He spotted us on the fairway. He summoned both of us and expressed his happiness at seeing two Allahabad boys playing golf, which was, unfortunately, acquiring the reputation of being an old man's game. He took us under his wing and trained us in the sport. I played it religiously in the initial years in Allahabad. Though I must confess, I do not pursue the game on a regular basis now.

I eventually took up other sports, organized picnics and parties, and mingled with more like-minded people in the city to create a life that I could celebrate every day. It was important not to make the cantonment my comfort zone, and so, I started interacting with the social fabric of the city. All such additional activities that made me happy contributed significantly to my performance at work in ways that can't be measured. It's a sin to burn in the hellish fires of business. Before you realize it, you will be consumed by its flames. Adding the right measure of colour will balance the scales and lighten you up.

Life is made up of myriad colours and colours light me up, literally. I was fortunate to train under eminent Bengali artist, Prakash Karmakar. He was heading the printing press and the design department at our Naini factory. Early training and my introspective nature keep me busy in the world of art. I collect art and am happy when new collectors reach out to me for advice. I am also honoured to be on the panel as a judge, year after year, at the Ravi Jain Annual Award presentation for upcoming artists. The show is hosted by Dhoomimal Art Gallery, Delhi. My training in art at the Brahmacharya stage, which led me to buy and sell art in the transactional stage of Grihastha, now keeps me fully involved and gives me the pleasure of sharing my knowledge at the transitional stage of Vanaprastha.

Going back to the army, another thing that I learnt from them was the equally strong and significant role women play in it. They are proud of their *fauji* husbands and create an environment which is beneficial for their career advancement. They devote their time to activities directed towards the welfare of the *jawans* and their families, besides nurturing their own children and preparing them for the real world. Their interpersonal skills are impressive. While it might look like I am over-analysing at this point, I still feel that it greatly changed my own understanding of the role of women or a spouse in life.

Sin 15: Not Acknowledging the Importance of Spouse

India is fast catching up with the West, and we see a lot of businesses being managed by educated and talented girls from within business families—the Biyanis (Future Group), the Reddys (Apollo Hospitals), the Sundaram Iyengars (TVS Group), the Chauhans (Parle) and the Godrejs, to name a few. Hence, I have used the gender-neutral term spouse. In a family business, we are always dealing with two sets—set A denotes the family and set B, the business. It is observed that in a large number of cases, while one spouse usually takes care of set A, the other one takes care of set B, and in sporadic cases, both take care of sets A and B. Whatever be the situation, the role of the spouse is vital in the family business. Hence, the importance of marrying right becomes indisputable.

India is a land of arranged marriages, but increasingly, children are making their own choices when it comes to a partner. Whatever choices they make, they need to consciously understand that a joint family business is full of conflicts. So, they should be marrying a conflict-solver and not a conflict-creator. Lack of interpersonal skills creates conflict. One must exhibit the right qualities and good behaviour while interacting with members of the family and also while interacting with outsiders on behalf of the family, an important characteristic one must look for in the spouse.

In my case, I was lucky. Meesha is mature, composed and possesses remarkable interpersonal skills. Both of us come from similar backgrounds, which became a big advantage. She grew up in a joint business family, had received a boarding school education and had a modern approach towards life. She saw a positive, well-coordinated working team in the elders of her family where her father, elder uncle and aunt (Bua ji) were first-generation partners. She was a bit surprised to see the conflicts in our family over geographical issues which are discussed further in Sin 18.

By the time we moved to Delhi to set up a new plant, we were already parents to two children, with the younger one being a year old. I had told her that if and when we did go to Delhi, she would be leaving behind the luxuries of the family home at Allahabad. I remember telling her jokingly about this change of role.

'Here, you are a *bahurani*. There you will be a *naukrani*. Are you prepared?'

Had it not been the same vision and common goal, any spouse would have retaliated against this step of changing the city of residence, especially with two young children. But Meesha was clear in her views. She was up to doing what needed to be done. Her background and upbringing helped us align our goals and what we wanted to achieve together. We must acknowledge that every spouse has a family she grew up in, her family of origin which influences her in her Brahmacharya. She carries those beliefs and values with her to her current family.

Spouses have their own aspirations and they respond to situations accordingly. Hence, their behavioural pattern can be broadly classified in the following manner.

Spouses

1. Who want to be set A (family)
2. Who want to be a subset of set A
3. Who want to be outside set A

Irrespective of the influences of the family of origin, it is the future they envision for themselves which determines their behaviour. This mindset also impacts future cohesiveness or conflicts within the family. None is right or wrong, the three must be understood and managed.

Spouses who want to be part of a family will use traditions and impose them strictly on others to achieve their position. Importance will be given to family over business. Their own importance is created by making members dependent on them, especially the younger ones. They will display a sacrificing nature and go to the extent of suppressing their own wishes for the larger good. They either become heads of the family or are lost in their pursuit of becoming one. They may not be conflict-creators but their actions can create a lot of conflicts. On the other hand, the ones who want to be a subset are a mix of the traditional and the modern.

These modern traditionalists will respect family values and traditions—business is first and so is the family. Irrelevant, meaningless and whimsical customs will be altered to suit their own beliefs. This approach gives them a distinct identity, in a positive way, within the joint family. They don't strive to be heads of the family. They show traits of a conflict-solver. That is the reason why they usually become the face of the family in society.

The third type exists only for the earnings of the business; they are not there for the family and its ways, and stay aloof, constantly displaying their displeasure. They may live separately and spend time creating their own identity in society, which is distinct from the family. They come across as conflict-creators, which they may not be. More often than not, their modernist/separative views are used for infusing conflicts.

While Meesha never entered the management of our business, I am elated to state here that she was my adviser and a key contributor to my achievements, a role she took immense pride in, as she always believed in business first. Giving the same importance to family, she was zealous about the education of my younger sisters and also dedicated herself towards building the future of our children. She chose the best schools for them, even going against my wishes. I had got our children registered in boarding schools when they were born—my son Rishi Raj in Mayo and daughter Veerangana in Welham's. They finally studied at Delhi Public School (DPS) at R.K. Puram, New Delhi.

I remember one incident when, Padma Bhushan recipient Dr Shyama Chona, the principal of DPS, our children's alma mater, had organized a session with the mothers of students. She, in her unique style, asked them about their work and roles as mothers. While most of them responded saying that they were lawyers, doctors or TV anchors, Meesha rose up to announce that she was a homemaker and was raising the biggest wealth of the family—our children—the future CEOs of our business. Whenever I recall this incident, even today, it gives me a sense of pride that Meesha always had her beliefs and priorities in place.

In the first generation, the role of the spouse is unavoidable. Most first-generation males agree that without the input and support of the wife, they would not have ventured into something new. While in the second and third generations, the norms of the family, family constitutions and various other factors determine the influence the spouse has on the family business.

I am tempted to mention Sanjay Kirloskar's wife, Pratima Kirloskar, here. Raised in a non-business family environment, she had the right mix of education, talent and family value system as the Kirloskars.

Pratima always had the capability to run a business but she never did since it was not the norm in the Kirloskar family back then to have women working in the family business. She accepted the situation and felt that if the business needed her and she was deserving, she would be asked to join anyway. Till then, she focused on set A—the family. In Pratima's own words, 'There are a finite number of formative years children have, say, fifteen. These precious fifteen years cannot be wasted away or lost to anything.' It is a concept we have already discussed in detail in this book under the Brahmacharya stage.

She also instilled two important qualities in the family—one, she kept the family positive, and two, she ensured clear communication between family members, something which seeped into the organization and its workings, eventually.

From the outside, she managed to communicate to the senior managers the concept of 'calibre over age', denouncing a dogmatic tradition of age being given preference over calibre and merit, which plagues old businesses and government bodies even today. So, as a spouse, she made it easy for her children to take on their roles in the family business.

Having a spouse with an isolated vision and aspirations can be a roadblock in the growth of the business and can become a sin that we create for ourselves. Hence, having the right partner with shared values and beliefs, is critical to the continuity and longevity of the family and the business.

Sin 16: Allowing Interference from the In-Laws

Let us step back a bit and refer to the two diagrams of sets A and B or the sets A, B and C. In a business family, the marriage of a son marks the expansion of set A. Marriage is a union of two individuals who start off on their Grihastha stage of life. It is important to understand that this young couple is a family unit by itself within the larger family. Effectively, the unit is a subset of set A and will, in due course, fall in or be a part of other intersections of the diagram. Parents raise their children as sons or daughters, though the daughters of the family are conscious of the fact that they will, eventually, become daughters-in-law of a new household.

Sons, on the other hand, are oblivious of the fact that they will be acquiring a new status. One rarely sees parents training their sons through childhood to play the role of a son-in-law. The attention this new status brings could be awkward for some but flattering for most. The son sees himself becoming a part of another family too. For the larger family, while the girl becomes their son's wife and a part of the family, her parents—the in-laws—don't. The new family unit may often take advice from the in-laws who are neither in set A nor in set B, which may be detrimental to the basic fabric of the joint family business.

How can one differentiate good advice from bad advice? Can advice be good for the young couple but bad for the family or vice versa? There is a thin line between what is good and what is bad. To be right, one must ensure that the advice is stemming from full knowledge of the subject, has an element of compassion and is communicated in the right frame of mind for it to be trusted. Advice with these ingredients is given in totality and is devoid of partiality. A person seeking advice must check its source and applicability given his/the circumstances.

Family businesses which are successful in managing families have something in common. They consciously create subsets at the time of marriage itself, giving the newly-married couple financial independence and a sub-identity. The young daughter-in-law is consciously made a traditional modernist. This keeps them joined to the hip with the other subsets of the family and issues are openly discussed within the family, avoiding blind dependence on the in-laws for advice.

Meesha's family had the coveted Maruti car agency in Bareilly. In the early stages, the company had allotted them multiple locations within India to operate from. The introduction of the Maruti car started a new chapter in the Indian economy. There was an emergence of a new class of consumers. National TV in 1982 and Maruti in 1983 were responsible for the rise of a strong consuming middle class in India. Maruti was tasting success with their common man's car. There was unprecedented demand and it led them to pressure their dealers to operate or surrender inoperative locations. My father-in-law spoke to my father and offered him the Lucknow agency.

My father was sure that 'he could not spare me', as he told my father-in-law in his own words that he would consider the possibility of taking it for the family. To that, my father-in-law candidly replied, 'Ram bhai, I am sorry to say that this offer is not for the family; it is for your son, who is my son-in-law.' I still remember my father's reaction—first a bit of a shock and then, his characteristic half-smile as reality dawned on him that apart from being his son, I was also someone's son-in-law.

It was crystal clear that the offer was not for the family. It also gave me a clear message that the offer was not for me but for his daughter's husband. This started off a very frank and fun relationship with my in-laws, which I cherish till date. All parents look out for their children who will always remain children in the eyes of parents, despite their age. Sometimes, this behaviour comes from their need to care and is very adorable. At other times, it stems from the need to control or interfere.

Parents of the spouse are natural advisers and guides to their children and are eager to help even when help is not needed. While they want the best, it can have the opposite effect too. The onus is on the children to understand the intention and the risk arising from it. Advice by in-laws, however legitimate, is based on how they perceive the family business and, subconsciously or consciously, in favour of the specific family unit comprising their daughter and son-in law. Completely overlooking the family hierarchy and its values, and deriving short-term benefits over long-term gains could disrupt overall business vision. Hence, a word of caution. Complete knowledge should be gathered before advising.

Good advice can lead to safety, security and prosperity, while bad advice can be destructive towards a family business.

Grandchildren benefit from close proximity of in-laws especially during their childhood (Brahmacharya) and maternal grandparents too influence and mould the next generation of business leaders. Exposure of the right kind can be an asset.

The in-laws can be an asset in a different scenario too. Their expertise or qualification may be required for business. Some families make the most of such opportunities. The long association of working with the family makes the in-laws feel like they are a part of it and they expect to be treated like any other family member, which may not always turn out as expected. This feeling of alienation can ultimately have an effect on the son and daughter-in-law. It is advisable to draw clear boundaries at the outset so that such situations do not arise. Many families ask me how they should deal with interfering in-laws. My response is, 'This situation cannot be handled individually and it is important to involve the daughter-in-law to put up a joint front in order to have open communication and define clear boundaries.' In one such case, where the family did not involve the girl, it took an ugly turn when the girl's parents turned the couple against each other.

Comprehensively, blind advice from in-laws shouldn't be taken for family business matters as subconsciously it will always be prejudiced towards their own son-in-law and daughter. This sin will be a roadblock in the growth and vision of the family, even leading to severe cracks.

To safeguard themselves from this sin, families must foster clearer communication with the parents of their daughter-in-law. Some families educate the in-laws about the family business, some even go to the extent of inviting them for sessions and meetings, as well as for family holidays. The objective, in such cases, is to reduce their insecurities about their daughter's future.

Sin 17: Not Creating a Formal Family Charter

'Do you have a family charter?' our professor asked us during a management class at the SP Jain Institute of Management and Research in 2000–01.

The unanimous reply was, 'No.'

He continued, 'Do you need one?'

The answer, again, was 'No.'

He asked each one of us the reason why we had said no to a charter and, based on our responses, he divided the class into three groups. Group one had all those students who claimed that their families had a happy, healthy and harmonious coexistence; charters were for families that had problems. The second group consisted of students living in small families that were bound together by a strong value system. They felt the need but feared that the charter might disturb their relationships.

The third and the largest group comprised students whose families were facing too many complications within, due to which there existed an atmosphere of suspicion and distrust. Such negativity gives rise to fear and birth to doubts regarding each other's intentions, thus creating apprehensions about formalizing anything on paper. That was a strong enough reason not to have a charter. A few from this group felt that they needed a charter but given the deteriorating conditions, the impossible task ahead was who would prepare it.

Unfortunately, this is how we are all conditioned to think. If the going is good, I don't need it. If the going is bad, I cannot have it even though I need it. The mind games continue. The reality is that every family has a charter. It could be verbal, or shrouded in customs. It could be coded, or just informal. All we need to do is formalize it. Let's understand the importance of doing it and why its significance increases for the third generation— Mahesh. The healthiest of families harbour minor irritations, personal frustrations, arguments and anger which are not out in the open. Some direction is needed before these become bigger in proportion and unmanageable. Hence, weighing the possibility of whether one needs it or not is not an option.

While early division is an ideal situation where you eliminate conflict and ensure continuity of families and businesses, there would be several businesses where division hasn't happened. Some businesses would be thriving in harmony, some running with conflict or chaos and some shut or on the verge of closure. If businesses could speak, they are likely to state in a chorus that the family may not feel the need for a charter, but going forward, it needs a code of conduct and needs to be under a charter. Going forward means growth and sustainability. The business may not be able to speak but it has a voice—its employees. From the senior management of a family company to a salesperson in a shop run by a family, all echo the same sentiment—if the family can manage themselves, the business can grow manifold.

Why can't families manage themselves? Why can't they be transparent, equitable and operate under predefined guidelines? Rules provide a stable environment and an opportunity for peaceful coexistence for members of a family. These protect all members and are a guide to achieving a common goal. Rules define what is expected of each member and what is not. All will agree that having rules and regulations help manage a family and these are better than being governed by the whims and fancies of elders. In the event that a family has multiple heads or none at all, there is no other option but to chart out a set of rules to manage the family.

If a formal charter is the panacea to all problems and applies to all members of the family, who is stopping it? Is it that the head wants to continue enjoying discretionary Powers over the family and the business that he himself does not want a charter? Or is it that the one who is enjoying Recognition as the representative of the family or the brand is feeling threatened? Some in the family enjoy additional Income and don't want this benefit to be done away with. Family members in the Management could be unwilling to exit and some owners may not want to disturb the current Equity status. Are they justified? No, they are only holding on to whatever they have. Something that keeps them relevant in the family business. Holding on gives them a false sense of security in a family business.

If early division has not taken place, and you are part of a family business that is operational and generating income, there is scope and hope. But the scope of managing the family and the hope of continuing a successful legacy—the business—will bear fruit only when all members of the family come together to minimize what I define as PRIME areas of conflict in a family business. The PRIME constitutes five important elements which influence continuity and survival of business and should be the main focus of any charter. These are:

1. **Power Struggle:** Power is when a person or a group of persons influence or execute on their own despite opposition. It is to be used to achieve a common business goal, but can be manipulated towards self-interest without regard for others in the family or the business itself. This is an area of conflict.

2. **Recognition and Fame:** Recognition of the creator, status of the family, fame of the company and power of the brand give anyone who may have no personal achievement, instant recognition and acceptance in the organization and society at large. When it is used for self-promotion at the cost of the family business, it creates conflict.

3. **Income:** Not receiving one's fair share of income from the family business is conflict enough.

4. **Management:** Managing the family business is a tough job and it has its perks too. When members don't contribute but want to be in the management just for the perks, it's a definite conflict creator.

5. **Equity (Ownership):** Ownership conflicts arise with unequal equity holdings by different verticals of a family.

Ayurveda broadly classifies diseases into two types. *Sadhya* (curable) diseases, which have cures and can be eliminated by attacking the root cause. *Asadhya* (incurable) diseases, which are difficult to eliminate, but their intensity can be reduced or even neutralized, if properly managed. These are mostly inherited, like asthma and diabetes, or are acquired due to faulty habits. If we draw a parallel between ailments and conflicts, the PRIME conflicts mentioned above have similarities with asadhya, the difference being ailments infect an individual while conflicts impact a family. Since there is no single cure or solution, the family, while still in their happy and harmonious state, must come together to address PRIME conflicts before they become destructive, and agree on a process to manage them. The family has to create a formal family charter to address all issues, both primary and secondary in nature.

It is equally important to have one where conflicts have already cropped up. An urgent sense of the need to survive must arise from within each member. The charter is the only next logical step in the family business, but it is easier said than done! It's the most difficult part to bring all family members together in the first place. You are dealing with bruises, hurts, suspicions, conspiracies and, most importantly, egos. In the first generation, there is business and no real recognition of the family. In the second, there is business and the family takes shape; it grows, strengthens its position and social standing. In the third, the social status of the family takes centre stage and starts to dominate and overpower the business, giving rise to false egos.

The family charter or a family constitution that is being proposed is nothing new. Every family, especially joint families, operate under a charter. In the early generations, it is usually all verbal and held together by emotional bonds and strong family values. Family conduct is based on their customs. Families are contained, everybody stays under one roof—the family house—and communication is good. The family knows how to interact in society on its behalf and for the sake of business, and rules are laid down by the founder(s) on how the family will interact with the business, as it is revered. Elders have a say and play a big role in ensuring that the family complies with the undocumented charter. We, as human beings, tend to get emotional quite often, which invariably leads to relationship issues; we resort to bickering too. These are kept within the four walls of the house and a conscious effort is made to keep the business insulated from all such personal issues.

As families grow in the second and, visibly, by the third generation, the all-formidable set A with its subsets A_1, A_2 and A_3 witnesses the emergence of verticals or branches of the family as shown in Figure 5 in Sin 6. It is natural for every newly-created branch of the family to expect recognition and get the opportunity to hold power. A tussle may arise if incomes and equities have variations between branches or subsets. Management of the business starts coming under the scanner. The undocumented charter starts to lose its shine and now holds little or no value. The family patriarch is not around, or too old and weak to ensure it is followed. By now, the family is no longer facing functional issues or petty disputes. It's the start of conflicts of identity, income and an invested future. These conflicts are PRIME and can no longer be limited to the four walls of the house. They move away from the house and towards the business. The battle between the members is played out in boardrooms and business becomes the battleground, threatening its core existence.

It is time to address the PRIME. It is high time to have a formal family charter. Businesses that have travelled into the third generation have done things right in the first two. The onus is now on the third generation to do something good by responding to challenges to ensure continuity for themselves and their future generations. The first generation created the business; the third has to create a family.

This is the real test for Shiva (Mahesh), instead of living on the edge (unpredictable). Instead of performing the dance of destruction, taandav, it is time to manifest as Shankar, the destroyer of darkness. It is time to become the eliminator of doubt, discord and disorder, to recreate a world where there is transparency, trust, mutual respect and a conscience.

He has to collect disparate members and recreate the identity of the family, having a common goal of a successful legacy called business. If a creator must create, the destroyer will destroy. My visualization of the taandav to be enacted by the third generation is for the disruption of the existing mindset. He has to do the dance of disruption and create a new order for the third and subsequent generations. He disrupts, not destroys. If he cannot disrupt, the prevailing situation will destroy the family business.

The Pilibhit Sugar Mill was in its third generation and the fourth generation had been inducted already. There were seven members in the fourth generation, building immense pressure on the finances of the business operations of the two units, leading to negative profitability. The patriarch, Madho Prashad, a friend of my father, was flooded with suggestions to sell one of the two operating units of the sugar mill to meet the financial requirements of the family. One other suggestion was to recall the services of the expert in the sugar business who had helped them earlier. Madho Uncle, a diminutive man in his Vanaprastha, sat in his palatial bungalow in Nainital and thought out of the box. He knew that these solutions were temporary. It was time to transform the mental set-up of the family from thinking like a family business to behaving like a business family. With the help of the same sugar expert, R.P. Nevatia, he identified one member from the family who had the capability to manage business operations by himself on behalf of the family. Willing to disrupt the status quo, he mandated that everyone else including him would exit the management. He managed to break the curse!

Today, the sugar business is profitable, no mills have been sold. With ownership in place and steady incomes flowing in, most members have diversified into businesses they were passionate about. There is peace and prosperity as the division between ownership and management is well-defined. I reached out to the person who was chosen to run the operations, who is also a friend. I was keen to know from him the reasons for success. What I gathered from him is that the business was never really the problem. The problem was the family. Actually, not even the family, but the PRIME conflicts plaguing it. I couldn't agree more with him. To get business to grow, family issues have to be addressed first. After the business got on track, he himself exited the management, leaving behind a healthy company in the hands of a CEO and his professional team of managers to take it forward for the family–owners. He was happy about the turnaround, but there was one thing he was fearful of. He told me, 'Ajay, the family constitution is still verbal. That's the only thing that worries me.'

At Baidyanath, the second generation took another look at the existing charter. They upgraded it to ensure continuity of business structures and operations, taking into account the advent of the third generation. The sin that we suffered was not formalizing it. It was, again, merely verbal. Hence, when events did not go as per plan for any member, it was easy to undo and disobey the charter. The second generation should have made a formal charter, clearly laying down guidelines on the business as well as the family front; on how to make decisions, solve problems, the methodology to be adopted for resolving conflicts and the modalities of governing the business.

The charter on the business front governs issues like constitution of the board of directors, succession, induction of family members in the business, remuneration and dividend payouts. On the family front, it addresses the education expenses of family members, marriages, charity, investments and more such tangible and intangible issues like legacy and goodwill. On a lighter note, I am quite sure that this book, full of my experiences, would not have happened if the second generation at Baidyanath would have created a timely formal charter.

Family businesses that are afloat in the mature stage have their own strengths. While the Pilibhit family addressed the concerns of the family (set A) as it was the third generation who was willing to go ahead with the disruption, we at Baidyanath had a dedicated second generation set of members who were focusing on managing the business (set B) with the belief that if the business was taken care of, the family would be taken care of too. Alas, that is not true. In such cases, managing the family part of the family business becomes key, especially when the family tree is growing more branches and sub-branches.

With the increase in the number of inheritors, our second generation decided to part-transfer their shares in the company to the third generation and, in some verticals, to the spouses. This created new business owners. The existing verbal charter of the family wasn't addressing the real needs of the third-generation owners, leave aside the requirements of the spouses who were now owners. In fact, it had not taken such possibilities into consideration at all. While in the second generation, most of the family was involved in the business; by the third, most owners were not involved in its management. They had less direct information about the affairs of their own company while some did not even access the premises.

Whatever said, a non-working family member, who has the ownership and emotional stake in the family business, cannot be ignored. Natural differences started appearing between working and non-working owners, not to forget some artificially created differences. To address these PRIME concerns and move ahead, the family made multiple attempts to come together to restructure the business which would include the formation of a formal charter that could address the increasing number of owners in the family. While most could see the benefits of this move, some were still trying to comprehend the ownership dimension. A few became so wary of it that they began to fear it. They had a feeling that something unpleasant was being shoved down their throats. Finding humour in the uncertainty, some members nicknamed it the Magna Carta. The fear of the unknown and the uncertainty of losing whatever one was holding on to, kept overtaking all logic and rationale.

Under 'Size of Family Business', a chapter earlier in the book, we discussed that in the global scenario, India has a large number of family businesses in their third generation—the mature stage, a nomenclature given by business analysts. We also discussed the reason why these businesses are in their third or fourth generations. These Indian businesses, that started generations ago, now have large families that are extremely diverse in their compositions. A closer look at these families reveals a complex maze of multiple generations with each generation having its members in various stages of life (Brahmacharya, Grihastha, Vanaprastha and Sanyas). This is intermixed with parents and siblings, uncles and aunts, cousins and second cousins. This diversity means different behaviours, attitudes and mindsets. Such kind of heterogeneous composition of families can no longer be kept together only with emotional values or verbal commitments and promises. Differences are bound to crop up.

The fabric of the family changes due to births and deaths, marriages and divorces, and hence, the dynamics of this complexity cannot be contained in sets A and B as it has more to do with the distinction between owners and managers than between the family and the business. The three-set diagram, as shown in Figure 2, comes into play to deal with such complexities and should form the basis of the creation of any family charter. Needless to say, each family might have unique needs and requirements from its family charter and it must be created accordingly.

Coming back to our family and similar business families who are joined at the hip, I have noticed another interesting phenomenon as to why members are hesitant to form a charter. It stems from familiarity. While on one hand, familiarity breeds contempt, resulting in challenging and painful interactions among members, it also provides them with a sense of security.

Family members develop skills to manage (manipulate) each other and become comfortable living in a herd. They may argue or fight, but they also derive their strengths from each other. For some, the fear of disturbing the support system becomes another stumbling block in the formation of a charter, while for others, it is losing control over the environment and members.

This is the fear of the unknown, when on the contrary, a charter does away with uncertainties amongst family members and gives them their rights, safety and security. Without a charter, one is restricted by obligations and the hierarchy of the larger joint family. There is no distinction between a family member (set A) and a family–owner (set C). There are rapidly fading lines between a manager, a family member working as a manager and an owner–manager, a distinction that needs to be more profound. Family resources remain locked and the next/third generation is not allowed to take advantage of them to branch out on their own. Families don't grow the business they are managing because it does not belong to them solely. Whoever has whatever little power starts to wield it—a crab-in-a-bucket mentality (meaning 'If I can't have it, neither can you') develops in the family. The choice is to let the family play out a new episode of a family soap opera, just like on TV, or to question one's fears and create order out of the chaos.

Larger families tend to waste too much time on secondary conflicts while it's the PRIME that needs more attention. Hence, the charter must clearly address PRIME conflicts in detail. We all know that it is impossible to completely eliminate PRIME conflicts though secondary conflicts could be fully annihilated. The success of the charter is measured by checking to what extent it can minimize PRIME conflicts.

Professional help should be sought from subject matter experts to build a charter. They must be given the right mandate. After all, they are not the conscience keepers of the family. The family must be prepared to break existing rules—yes, *unjustified ones*. The ones that do not address common concerns. Irrelevant family customs. Old habits that are played up under the garb of family culture. They must use their own wisdom and the experience of other families to create this rulebook while establishing the difference between what is justified and what is not.

Charters are also necessary where families have divided the business and live separately, but operate their companies under a common family name. They may stand separated, but are bound together and obligated to safeguard and grow the intangible asset of a family name. Some families customarily live together while running separate businesses. They, too, must consider a charter before generational behaviour takes centre stage.

Now, let us consider another scenario where businesses are not running; incomes have dried up and the family is left with closed factories, land and machinery. This is not a business conflict, but more simply put, it is a division-of-asset conflict and should be dealt with accordingly. The key question that needs to be answered while considering the division of assets is, does the family want to make an equal division, or does it want to bring in the emotional quotient and play fair? Being fair means letting your own emotional side overpower your practical one.

Solutions lie in an equal division. Being fair, as virtuous as it may sound, gives weightage to emotional factors while dividing; typical examples being elder versus younger child; capable versus incapable child; successful versus unsuccessful child, etc. This will create further conflicts, resulting in delays which may remain unresolved even in future generations. The answer, my friend, is blowing in the wind.

To sum up, if early division has not happened, a formal family charter must come into effect. Whatever be the generation, the contents of the charter have to be formal—specifying the steps and processes. It has to be legal and binding on all members of the family, though, in reality, it is the intent of each member which keeps the charter strong.

Sin 18: Getting the Next Generation to Inherit Conflict

As mentioned earlier, our business had five demarcated geographical zones to ensure smooth operations. I need to go back in time to explain this sin, when the third-generation successors, chosen to represent the family, were settling in the business and effectively coordinating with each other. We were learning new techniques of business from our younger uncles and utilizing the wisdom and experience of my father and other uncles. This interaction initiated by the third generation increased communication within the second generation, which had been dwindling over time. There was harmony across. The third generation was doing fine with the family business and the projects they had undertaken under the diversification plan were all on track. I would wonder why there was such a negative perception about the third generation.

Uttar Pradesh (UP), a large state, was divided in two geographical zones. The area between eastern and western UP, from Bareilly to Kanpur including the capital Lucknow, was common to the two verticals operating in UP. The vertical managed by my father was operating in the east while my uncle who was running operations in the west made way for my younger uncle and his son to manage the vertical. His son and I were closer in age and we shared a good bond as cousins. A bonhomie that would later translate into a working advantage.

The joint operation of seven districts was not a business-friendly arrangement, but in a joint family business a lot of situations exist for reasons known only to the earlier generations. The new management, with a business approach, was not happy with this arrangement. It became a conflict. Matters needed to be ironed out as my father knew it to be a case of misinformation. All logic based on family arrangements yielded no results; we reached a dead end.

Our family had always followed a two-step methodology of resolving conflicts within the business. Direct communication was encouraged as the first step. The involved parties had to resolve their differences mutually. No other family member was encouraged to intervene. It helped the disputing parties to arrive at a consensus on their own, which was voluntary. Not getting anywhere with the first step, my father opted for the second—the family forum. Experience had taught him that all issues could be settled at such a forum. He found this to be a more effective way since the solution had the concurrence of the family. So, he requested for a family meeting.

There is a vast difference between a dispute and a conflict. The former are smaller issues that can be settled easily between two parties, but the latter are of a bigger nature and need the intervention of arbitrators. It was clear that the claim over the geographical area was not a dispute but a conflict.

The larger family tried to reason a solution, but nothing seemed to be working. No justification or logic was making any sense. The meeting was heading nowhere and I could see my father's trust in the forum being shaken. I broke all protocols and went to the extent of even proposing a division of the alleged disputed area to end the feud there and then. With a failed arbitration, the next thing we saw was the new management selling goods in our clearly demarcated geographical areas with the intent of exerting pressure on us to give up joint ownership of the areas totally in their favour.

This happened because the family charter that existed was undocumented and ran on trust, faith and time. It was not legally binding and hence, had scope for interpretations and eventually, conflicts related to Ownership of areas cropped up.

I went up to my father and asked if we should relinquish our rights on the area and just let go to maintain peace. I was witness to the unreasonable discussions at the family meeting and their tone and pitch disturbed me. Further, it was a given that the move of selling goods in each other's territories would affect brand equity. This was the first time that my childhood fear that the third generation was responsible for destroying everything reared its head and stared at me!

'No, it has nothing to do with the third generation; the issue pertains to the second.' I tried to reason and console myself. But I was fully aware that even though the issue was between adults of the older generation, the brunt would have to be borne by us. As businessman and politician Herbert Clark Hoover said, *Older men declare war. But it is the youth that must fight and die.*

My father could see me visibly upset given my fears surrounding the third generation curse and secondly, because of a strong bond I shared with my cousin, I was adamant not to let anything dent our relationship. In an effort to convince me, my father suggested that we could bury the conflict but it would not do any good since it wouldn't be a permanent solution and would turn around to bite the next generations.

Disputes can originate in any generation. If left unresolved, they are inherited by subsequent generations. Disputes which pass on to the next generation become inherited conflicts and have the potential to destroy the business. The label of destroyer could be pinned to any generation; it's just that the complexities are the highest in the third.

'Ajay,' my father said, 'one thing that you need to make sure of is that your sons should inherit the business, not the conflicts.' He explained further, 'The sooner you resolve a conflict, the better it is!' Clearly, the ill-feelings and hurt left behind by delaying a solution diminish when it is solved early. He continued, 'Unfortunately, conflicts do not get resolved themselves; a lot of effort has to be put in to do it.' I did remember the initial efforts put in by us and, subsequently, the larger family, but all to no avail. He then asserted that to solve the conflict, we might have to go to any extent.

'I have complete confidence in you,' he told me. We then planned an obvious counter-strategy and entered their clearly demarcated area, thus creating an unethical business war.

I must reiterate that we made one last-ditch effort, asking for withdrawal from our areas of operation, or else we would be forced to retaliate, the consequences of which were known to all.

Grihastha is the toughest stage of life and does create warlike situations. In our case, it actually became a war. It was clear by now that my father, a man of principles, was not fighting an area conflict, but a value conflict. Unfortunately, a value conflict is the most difficult. Values are strong, so is the stance. Ours lasted for a decade. The final outcome was that we got a larger area of operation than what was originally disputed. The objective was achieved. With clear demarcated territories, both the verticals got down to reconstruct all damages. We put the conflict, which had impacted our profitability and peace of mind, behind us. It was time to move ahead. War does strange things to people; it honed my battle skills and gave me a different kind of exposure. It was the next level in the university of experience.

Value conflicts have a tendency to stretch over time and result in higher distrust and alienation of warring parties, giving rise to relationship conflicts. In our case, there could have been relationship issues between my uncle and my father, further inherited by my cousin and me. In all probability, we could have passed it on to the next generations. The elders were not affected because of the strong family values they were raised with, and both had very distinct positive personalities. Childhood bonds built due to the networking of cousins helped my cousin and me to manage this conflict so that neither of us emerged badly hurt and the relationship too did not suffer. We spoke about our role as conflict-solvers for the larger good of the family and I never let this spoil my relationship or use it as a reason to harbour any ill-feelings towards my cousin. It was primarily because I knew this was a promise to the family that we had to keep, more like a duty that we had to fulfil, to resolve a family conflict. This positive approach also ensured no negative comments from either party. Today, our children enjoy the best of relationships; my cousin and me are proud of the fact that as parents we both did not make our children inherit conflicts.

Legacy is passed on as a narrative of events in a family business. One grows up listening to stories of how it all started. Of achievements and disappointments. Of what actually happened and what could have happened for the good or bad. Everyone has a story to tell—the cook, the chauffeur, family elders, neighbours and society. It becomes very difficult to separate people's personal opinions from real facts. At times, parents tell false narratives to their children to cover their failures.

In the event of a conflict, one is informed only of one side of the story to keep the numbers up and strong. Even if you want to know the other side of the story, it may not be readily available or made accessible to you. This is done because it is very easy to take a side and stick by it when you know only one half of the family. One-sided stories are also identity markers. They create stereotypes and are incomplete. There could be falsehood packed as truth or just half the truth. This is the worst kind of inherited conflict and should be avoided under all circumstances. The impact of such one-sided stories destroys the relationship between siblings and cousins for no fault of theirs.

To conclude, conflicts, when they reappear, are more volatile and cripple the organization. Hence, they cannot be passed on to the next generation, even if you have to go to the extent of a war.

I have never advocated war except as a means of peace.

—Ulysses S. Grant

Sin 19: Breaking Away from the Family Charter/ Going Against the Family Charter

When the bugle had been silenced and peace was restored, our vertical was allocated a larger geographical area to work with, bringing in increased profitability. Advantage to the vertical was further strengthened by the new plant I had set up near Delhi. The victory, my success in setting up the new plant, and my marketing aggressiveness made customers and society see me as the face of the company. There was appreciation within the family too.

This created a conflict of Recognition. Everyone deserved a share of the glory. All the siblings were no longer content with being family–owners. Nothing could stop all from being part of the day-to-day Management and becoming family–owner–managers. The authority of the patriarch and the safety cover the charter promised seemed to have come to naught. The message on the wall was loud and clear.

Breaking the charter can wreak havoc in any family business; in our case it was a complete disaster. Siblings started scrambling for work to justify their presence and usefulness in the business. My authoritarian father had not lost sight of his vision to professionalize the organization and move the family out of day-to-day operations. His advisers had briefed him so and he was convinced that this was the panacea to the illness his children were suffering from. His crack team, which included me, was already on the job in Delhi to fulfil his vision. In the short-term, based on each one's strengths, he delegated focused responsibilities to the rest of the family members. He divested part of his Equity to his four sons to bring about a sense of security around the family units. Positive vision leads to positive actions.

The family shared a proposal to start operations in the US. Sensing an opportunity there, my father agreed. He announced that the project was to be headed by my brother. The headquarters were to be at Dallas. It had a sizeable market of Indians, his mother-in-law, who lived there, would be a support and, to top it all, our elder sister and her husband were running a successful cosmetics manufacturing business out of Dallas. The family appreciated their achievements and were sure that their guidance could prove helpful. My mother had a lot of confidence and faith in my sister's presence.

America witnessed the most morbid attack on its soil on 9/11—the incident shook the world. It was the night of 9 September 2001 in Delhi. We were having an early farewell dinner for my friend from Cayman Islands, who was leaving for New York that night. The TV was on and suddenly, my wife drew our attention towards the screen. We were witness to the second aircraft hitting the second tower (the images flash back with such clarity whenever I think of it).

On that fateful morning, two planes hit the twin towers of the World Trade Center in New York, but across the globe, millions of human minds were hit by shock. Terror and grief filled every heart. It had an effect on us too. My brother had to move back to India with his family, to safer environs. That was the end of our American dream.

The evacuation happened so quickly that there was no clear plan or direction. With my brother's return, we noticed some alterations in my father's grand vision of moving himself besides the business to Delhi. We could see a slowing down of the entire process. These deviations were not sending positive signals to the professionals. With uncertainty in the air, the senior management started leaving the company. With no heads of departments, we started dividing the departments amongst us brothers for individual control.

It didn't end there. Each started resorting to power play, leading to poor communication between the departments. We suffered a serious blow in coordination and synergy of the business due to increasing personal differences and decreasing business communication. This was definitely a conflict of management. This was the second time that I came face-to-face with my childhood fears. This time, it started affecting me, especially when we reached a point where different departments started having different company holidays! I could see the curse manifesting.

Families with an experience of witnessing their charter being broken will agree that it can be devastating. It is a calamity which comes uninformed and leaves a trail of destruction in its wake.

Human resilience is amazing and comes in all forms. While the conflict of management between us brothers was on, our father was experiencing a personal low at that time. He lost his best friend and younger brother, BK, his elder brother, BL, and his dear Maa within a span of six months. These three people were his invisible immunity, his support and strength. Leaving his personal loss behind, he gathered himself to clean up the prevailing situation in the management of the business, solve disputes amongst siblings, equalize income and apportion responsibility along with authority to each son. We were married and with children and he could see us as sub-units of his family. He wanted a new, unique charter for his own vertical. Two verticals had already designed their own charters, as sub-branches of the family had emerged within these verticals as well.

It was the summer of 2008. He invited the whole family to his summer retreat at Naukuchiyatal, a serene nine-cornered lake, in Nainital district. He had built this house to get away from the now-overcrowded Nainital town. Here, he had the luxury of playing host to a greater number of people. He was magnanimous. Family and friends can vouch for this. With his confidant Colonel Sharma by his side, he summoned us to the living room and announced the formation of a family council. This time around he executed a formal document and got us all to sign on the dotted line. This document would be the foundation on which the family charter was to build. It was the only way to eliminate the prevailing PRIME conflicts.

The way governance used to work in each branch of the family in the first and second generations was through a patriarch. With newer generations and an increasing number of stakeholders with spouses from different cultures, faiths and economic backgrounds, our family was adopting a new attitude—the concept of one supreme patriarch was no longer effective. This new setting would only invite more politics and chaos. A patriarch, a living human being, is vulnerable to manipulations. It is advisable to replace his position as the sole decision-making authority by a family charter which controls and governs the family. But wherever a charter is being prepared, there are members who do not want it and they indulge in delaying tactics. They do not want to be governed equally; they don't want clear rules because they want to have their way by manipulating the patriarch. They are experts at that. Unfortunately, we experienced this too.

It's crystal clear that undocumented charters are easily broken. It is recommended to have charters documented and legally binding. Charters are made for the benefit and continuity of the family business. They address issues that are generational and intergenerational; between family units, and between individuals. They are applicable to all members, treating them equally. Then why is the formation of a charter delayed, or alternatively, why is a charter broken and who breaks a charter?

One simple trait—a sense of entitlement—is the villain. Anyone can harbour this feeling. A person suffering from this actually believes that he deserves more than his peers. This unjustifiable expectation is backed by an arrogant demand. He does not respect merit and the word equality is alien to him. This is the single largest cause for delay or breaking up of the family charter by a family member.

The second inherent characteristic is a big ego. The 'I', 'Me', 'Myself' syndrome. Ego is an illusion which keeps you away from reality. It builds a false narrative of the 'I' always being right. One stops trusting others; leave alone believing in them, listening to them or learning from them. In fact, you start resenting others. The ego stops you from wishing well for them; it even makes you want to harm them. You become heartless and compassionless and want to feel superior to everyone around you. Ego is something that makes you lose the power of thinking rationally and wisely for the self, family or the business. Ryan Holiday, in his book *Ego is the Enemy*, writes, 'The ego we see most commonly goes by a more casual definition: an unhealthy belief in our own importance. Arrogant. Self-centred ambition . . . It's that petulant child inside every person, the one that chooses getting his or her own way over anything or anyone else.'

Self-entitlement and a big ego are the two most common reasons that result in a family member breaching a charter. Families that can see any member having a combination of both these characteristics must address it on priority or be prepared for the destructive taandav. Identifying members having these traits and keeping them at a safe distance from the management is a recommended step to safeguard the family business.

'What can you do to promote world peace? Go home and love your family,' said Mother Teresa. The charter not only binds but defines the family. Families move beyond just being an emotional attachment. They solidify to become institutions in themselves, just like any club, association, forum or chamber that we are a part of as members. A group of diverse people coming together for a common interest governed by a set of rules applicable to all the members. The differentiation between a family and family–owners mentioned in a charter truly transforms a family business into a business family—a family beyond just the bond of blood, a network of people who take joy in each other's company. Lee Iacocca said, 'The only rock I know that stays steady, the only institution I know that works, is the family.' Charters have the power to transform crumbling sandstone into solid rock. In such a scenario, if a member is attempting to break a rule, he is effectively breaking a family and destroying an institution, the fallout of which can be no business and no family.

The million-dollar question is, 'How do you ensure that no one breaks the charter?' After all, we have often heard that rules are made to be broken. It is wise to understand the difference between flouting a rule and breaking or bending it. As humans, we all, at some point, flout or tend to disregard a rule. Without getting into the psychology of this action, let us stick to our objective of adherence to a charter. A charter is a self-created rulebook by the family, for the family. To avoid any misadventure, it is advisable to keep one set of functional rules standardized across members. The other set should be codified, collectively prepared to maintain discipline within the family business. Codified rules should carry penalties and fines if tampered with.

If at any point of time, the family, its arbitrators, or the family governance council feels the need to bend a rule, it clearly means that the rule has outlived its purpose. Then, yes, it needs to be broken and modified to suit the current requirement. We know that a part of the governance implemented by the charter is indeed engraved in stone. Yet, a part of it will remain dynamic and open to change as time and situations demand. This flexibility is critical to avoid the charter from becoming obsolete. Hence, if there is a situation in the family that the sanctity of the charter is in danger, rather than letting any member break it, it is advisable to bring the issues to the table, discuss them openly and modify the charter collaboratively.

In our case, the charter was broken for individual aspirations, which is a sin. It should have been discussed by the entire family and modified to suit the needs of the business.

Sin 20: Not Upgrading Oneself

The first stage in the journey of life is based on how one's parents coach and educate them. Brahmacharya is devoted to infusing knowledge and honing skills to apply and use them in life. Parents envision a future and the role that the child will play in that future and work towards improving their offspring's core abilities along the way. Some families do it very methodically and diligently; some out of responsibility towards their children, while some do it under societal pressure. In the eastern cultures, it is viewed as parents 'discharging their duties'. How many of us are part of the future our parents envisioned and trained us for? One may be fortunate, but does the future remain the same as envisioned years ago?

The world is changing constantly around us—work environments, technology, management skills, relationships, families, and just about everything. The question is, 'Am I to continue to be the person my parents trained me to be in my Brahmacharya?', or 'Am I to take responsibility upon myself in my Grihastha?' Most of us are shy to even approach this question; some like to remain in denial. While some may pose to be indifferent, the truth is that we all are improving and upgrading ourselves constantly. Self-improvement becomes more focused as we face challenges thrown at us during Grihastha. Upgrading oneself is the answer and it should consciously become a part of life. It would be dumb to commit this sin.

The Delhi operations of our business were structured in a way that they were run by skilled and experienced professionals. An interesting topic of conversation in the family was that I, the family manager–owner, did not have an office to operate out of in the factory; instead, I functioned from an office in Delhi. At Baidyanath, the geographies were like little kingdoms managed from the forts (the factories) with the office of the owner touted as the durbar hall—a place from where the king presides and rules over his kingdom. That was a culture I was hell-bent on changing. The plant head had to be responsible towards his job and not stay in the shadows of the family. I had witnessed this happening at our Naini plant in Allahabad where the managers took credit for achievements and diverted the onus of non-achievements or bad decisions on the owner. For the smallest of things, they would run to the owner. I was adamant that feudalistic mindsets, which were non-progressive, would not be allowed to germinate here. Since we built the Delhi operations from scratch, we had a clean slate to start with and we could create our own culture and implement best practices.

The marketing head, who was from a multinational pharma company, was instrumental in implementing an impeccable work culture with modern systems and processes. The plant and the marketing office were functional and delivering the desired results. The new team was gaining from my experience and knowledge of the Ayurvedic industry and I was learning the skills they brought along. I would, sometimes, improvise on them too. I was being accepted as part of the team. I had finally upgraded myself from being the owner's son to owner–manager, adapting myself to working with skilled department heads.

Right up till the year 2000, multinational organizations were preferred over family businesses. It took the skilled workforce some time to open up to family-run businesses, when the economy was opening up and liberalization was the new buzzword. The IT boom was also just around the corner, what with the much-talked-about Y2K. Professionals considered family businesses as Lala[4] land and owners as Lalas, unlike today, when family businesses are seen as legacies and opportunities for successful turnarounds. That was all the more the reason why the thrill of accomplishment was satisfying. We had regular business meetings in which I noticed my shortcomings. While I would take the help of a paragraph to explain something, the subordinates were able to do it using just a phrase or by mentioning a theory or a law. These meetings started disturbing me.

The positive aspect of feeling disturbed is that it pushes you towards finding a solution to a problem, and one is forced to learn new skills and master new competencies. Feeling underqualified confirms the fact that you have room to grow. This feeling, once again, shakes you out of your comfort zone. It was then that I realized the importance of an MBA. I needed to understand business jargon to ensure that I was at par to deal with the people I was working with. With the determination to further upgrade myself, I started to explore the possibilities of doing an MBA. While the family was supportive, society wasn't.

---

[4]   A merchant or trader belonging to the trading community; viewed as old-fashioned with a non-progressive mindset.

Everybody said, 'Is thirty-five an age to go and study? You are the father of two children!'

The staff was also divided on my decision to study. I was battling the immediate need of managing the business versus my own self-development. The new team was well-qualified or had domain knowledge of Ayurveda and I could be spared. I discussed this with Meesha and she simply said, 'Ajay, your own development would eventually benefit the business. It is just a matter of time.'

SP Jain Institute of Management and Research (SPJIMR) had, just then, announced a new programme in management for owner–managers of businesses. This programme was designed for successful entrepreneurs in charge of family businesses who could study and look after the business simultaneously. The programme didn't require me to be present on campus all the time, and I could juggle between my business and my learning. I must confess that acquiring knowledge was fun, but implementing it in a joint family business was tough and challenging.

Such programmes and institutes have a lot of takeaways. We were all experienced owner–managers with pretty much the same business backgrounds and facing similar challenges. Acquiring knowledge and providing solutions became so robust that we all continue to stay connected and lend our wisdom and learnings to each other, even today. The other advantage of a good business school is that the professors continuously keep loading you with information, and in the process, your knowledge and skills get upgraded. I am thankful to the institute for the learnings, experience and the friendships it brought me.

One person with whom I developed a great bond at SP Jain was Shishir Nevatia, the owner of Sunjewels Private Limited. Sunjewels works with leading brands and retailers worldwide to produce fine jewellery.

Shishir's son, Kapil, while planning to pursue his management course from SP Jain in Mumbai, came across the owner–manager programme. An existing family business faces a lot of challenges, some of which were not new to Kapil.

So, the youngster approached his father, asking him to consider attending the programme. Shishir joined the course. It was indeed encouraging to see the son, who was in his early twenties, and his father, who was in his late forties, both pursuing two different courses in the same institute for the betterment of their business and to secure their future.

Shishir, a strong practitioner of yoga, would propagate it, besides institutional education and acquisition of requisite business knowledge and management skills. Yoga offered Shishir the mental and physical strength—two important attributes that are necessary for a manager to successfully navigate the challenges of doing business on a daily basis. Yoga is a science and one must master this skill for fitness of both the mind and body as the two are important to cope with stress levels of the corporate world on a day-to-day basis.

According to a recent survey conducted by Cigna TTK Health Insurance,[5] about 89 per cent of the population in India says they are suffering from stress compared to the global average of 86 per cent. Stress builds up when we are unable to cope. And we cannot cope as we don't have the skills. The prescription to deal with stress is upgradation of skills.

Shishir Nevatia is also a staunch supporter of spirituality and often told us, 'How you lead your life is how you do business.' Ethics and morality in business are strong factors due to which family businesses survive through generations. Through yoga and spirituality, Shishir taught us what they don't teach you in business schools. This reconfirmed my belief that an individual should not just upgrade himself through education or self-skills, but also continuously strive to evolve as a human being.

Incidentally, eight years later, in 2008, Shishir went on to do

5   https://economictimes.indiatimes.com/magazines/panache/89-per-cent-of-indias-population-suffering-from-stress-most-dont-feel-comfortable-talking-to-medical-professionals/articleshow/64926633.cms

the Owner/President Management (OPM) course at Harvard Business School and I wasn't surprised.

In family businesses, family members have authority which is rarely challenged by subordinates; family members are over-involved in minor day-to-day activities, leaving no time for themselves. Sycophancy doesn't allow them to realize the need to upgrade themselves. Many have asked me how it is possible to know that one needs to upgrade oneself. It is very individualistic. However, the following three scenarios are sure pointers to think of beginning the upgradation process:

+ The feeling of being under-skilled
+ The people you are working with scare you
+ The feeling that people will leave the organization

Family members in their Vanaprastha or even in their late Grihastha are proud of the experiences they have acquired. They feel frustrated when it is considered irrelevant by young managers with new skills. Wisdom is a culmination of experiences and should never be discarded. Knowledge can be gained inside a classroom, but wisdom is always gained outside. The success of family businesses lies not in abandoning these rich experiences one has gained but finding new ways to apply them. You have to wed the two!

Sin 21: Not Growing the Pie

If you remember the ownership chart we created in Brahmacharya, with each generation, the number of owners increases, reducing the income of an individual. Since there are more mouths to feed, the share of what each one takes home reduces.

In Baidyanath, early division didn't happen and the pie was not large enough to be divided further. Pressure was building up and everyone was tense since it was clear that more dissatisfied owners would soon be ready to claim what they considered was theirs and the family would be left with no other option but to sell out, something that the entire family was against. The vision was common, the entire family unanimously agreed that selling out was not an option.

The only way to work around this was to increase the size of the pie so that the earning per share didn't shrink any further and every member received increased Income. This concept was propagated and advocated by my youngest uncle—R.K. Chacha ji. He had introduced this idea to the family quite sometime ago. Finally, the time arrived when the family came together. We realized that to break the curse, we had to move ahead—increase the pie—for which it was necessary to professionalize the company and ensure a smooth exit of the family from the management.

The biggest challenge was to stop working as five verticals and bring them together to operate as one. We needed the right consultants to execute this job and it took six long, exhausting months to finalize the agency. It was Ernst & Young Global Limited which was finally hired to take up the job to facilitate the process of transformation from five independent, family-run verticals to a professionally operated company with an aim of increasing the pie.

EY initiated a dialogue with different verticals discreetly to understand their insecurities and concerns if they had to exit the management. Based on that, it was EY's job to address all those pain points and create a robust family charter. Unfortunately, it collapsed. The reason was Equity.

It so happened that my eldest uncle passed away when the second generation was at the helm, and the third generation was not introduced to the business. The second generation allocated my uncle's position on the board to my cousin and started treating him as part of the second generation itself. But he was from the third generation with third generation issues on his mind. So, when we were signing the papers and looking forward to popping the champagne to celebrate the successful transition in the EY office in Gurgaon, issues were raised for clarification from the second generation. With no answers in sight it was natural for the process to stop.

Madhav Shriram, MD of DCM Shriram Industries Limited with their flagship company, Daurala Sugar, rightly calls himself a second-generation businessman, as his father, Lala Bansi Dhar, exercised an early division within the larger Shriram Group (popularly known as the DCM Group). If the early division had not happened, Madhav would be dealing with fourth-generation issues, while now the onus on him is to plan for the family's third generation.

He feels that when there is not enough to divide, then '. . . in any family, it's important to first sit down and answer a simple question: Do we want to work together, or, more importantly, can we work together?'

On a black-and-white trajectory of division or work together, Madhav interestingly offers a 'work together to divide' option. This means working together to increase the pie to a pre-defined goal which allows members of the family to embark on individual journeys. While this solution has immense potential to solve a lot of prevailing issues, Madhav cautions families who opt for this option. 'There is no room for history,' he emphasizes. 'Historical issues in the family have to be left behind as these will become roadblocks on the way forward.'

Growing the pie translates into 'more for everyone'. Family businesses embark on a plan to grow the pie with the sole intention of creating more income for the family. In case the charter demands it, one can create work opportunities for the family too. Some families invest and assist their members in diversified businesses to generate more earnings. If the mood is positive, opportunities are immense. In a family business, when positivity eludes itself and there is an income conflict, it is normal for the family to ask someone to give up a slice of their pie in favour of the other. This is settlement by redistribution of the pie. This generates negative reactions and solutions are far from achievable. Growing the pie is a positive action. Sometimes, there are situations wherein we talk about expanding the pie. This should not be confused with growing the pie. Expanding the pie is adding value during the negotiation processes.

An owner or promoters can only increase the family pie with contributions to the topline (turnover) and the baseline (profit). To save costs and provide work opportunities, many families induct members from the next generation as managers in a quick-fix solution. These members may not always be suitable for the role in the existing business or have the right skills to deliver the best results. Hence, such an action often turns out to be counter-productive and becomes a major cause for PRIME conflicts. Due diligence is a must on the route being adopted to increase the pie.

When the core issue in the third generation was continuity of business and increment in incomes, we were not dejected by the failed attempt. Failure can be debilitating. It can make you give up on your goals and dreams. Being unsuccessful is often temporary, but giving up and not attempting it again makes it permanent. Not to be disappointed, we decided to implement a similar professionalization exercise with the verticals that could come together to do the same.

Sin 22: Eliminating Secondary Conflicts

Eliminating PRIME conflicts completely is utopian and a rare occurrence. One can work to neutralize and manage these PRIME conflicts. In their shadow, there are multiple layers of secondary conflicts. They are not derivatives of the PRIME; instead, they fan their fire. They drain one's time and energy and become obstacles in the way of minimizing PRIME conflicts, as also impediments in the growth of the family business on a daily basis. Hence, they must be completely eliminated at all costs and at all levels.

Some of the examples of secondary conflicts are: living in the same house with common kitchens; making joint investments; cross-holding of shares; ownership of ancestral properties and the major one being family philanthropy. They could also arise out of a difference of values and upbringing in family members, or out of varying degrees of sentimentality and emotions. Lack of transparency also gives rise to conflicts. Any other conflict apart from the PRIME is to be considered a secondary one. Disagreements are considered healthy, but if there is a clash of interest, they convert into conflicts. Secondary conflicts can arise out of a situation or can be behaviour-related.

All families love each other and all families go through conflicts. It is difficult to rationalize them under categories. Family members are emotionally attached to each other. These create the first level of conflicts in family businesses. Second are definitely relationship conflicts given the regular interaction at home and in business. Sibling and generational rivalry are typically present across. The norms of the family create long-lasting conflict as customs and rules are broken to suit some members of the family. The ones who had to adhere to them feel cheated and carry grudges towards the members for whom customs were bent.

It might sound bizarre that philanthropy can be the cause of conflict, but it is cited as the most prominent secondary conflict reason as everyone has a different inclination. For example, the elder of the family might want to build a temple, while the third generation would want to work against global warming. Since these are not directly linked with business, it is best to divide the budget and let everyone follow their heart, thus eliminating this secondary conflict. Alternatively, it could be a planned activity entrusted to a group of family members who are not actively involved in the business. This group will also have the task of managing the budget towards social responsibility on behalf of the family, thus ruling out interferences from all family members. Where there is a successful business, there is philanthropy, and families devise varying methodologies to address it.

Often, there are families who live together but have separate businesses. In practice, they make a family constitution applicable for joint living and investment purposes. Families that cannot build a charter, at times, form a similar constitution at the family level to eliminate secondary conflicts. This provides a strong social status to the families leading to a host of opportunities and advantages.

In the event that a family charter is implemented, it automatically brings about transparency and discipline to protect family members from unnecessary secondary conflicts. It even designates members as arbitrators or a council of elders who would be taken into confidence to address any disputes or conflicts that might arise in the family.

Newer conflicts that arise with newer generations can be resolved by upgrading the family charter. Thus, the family charter, as mentioned earlier in the book, is constantly in upgradation and modification mode. Older families in India hold a lot of wealth as physical assets, which become a bone of contention when the family increases in number. Especially if such assets are not being utilized in an effective manner, it is best to divide them between family members or jointly put to productive use through a trust fund. Leaving them unattended will only lead to conflict of ancestral assets that is passed on to the next generation.

Family is a complex structure. There are members:

a) who are owners and in business;
b) who are owners but not in business;
c) who are not owners but in business; and
d) who are not owners and not in business.

The dynamics of relationships emerge out of this matrix, and so do secondary conflicts.

PRIME conflicts	Can be minimized by
Power	Creating the family charter
Recognition	Giving status to family members
Income	Growing the pie
Management	Bifurcating ownership and management
Equity	Early division
Secondary conflicts	**Creating a family charter**

* * *

Vanaprastha T3:
Figure 7

THIRD STAGE

STAGE	ASHRAM	4 Ts	GOAL
I	Brahmacharya	Training	Knowledge
II	Grihastha	Transaction	Wealth
III	Vanaprastha	Transition	Fame
IV	Sanyas	Turn-in	Relinquishment

Being from the third generation and managing our business, I am currently experiencing Vanaprastha. I have personally known multiple generations of many business families closely; I have witnessed accounts and incidents that have framed my theories and insights on this stage of life. It is one of the most critical stages and requires both attention and caution. Transition of business, knowledge, position or management from one generation to another is the soul of any family business. One thing that needs to be highlighted is that Vanaprastha is the transition where there is a handover of the management of the business and not ownership. The handover of ownership only happens in Sanyas, the last of the four stages.

Each generation is in a different frame of mind during their Vanaprastha. Hence, their behaviour and responses also vary. For the first one, it is very difficult to even accept this reality. They live with the ethos of death-do-us-part with business. The reason for this could be the feeling that the business is because of 'me', or the realization that there are not enough savings, or just an inherent need to reap more rewards, which does not allow one to give up. There are numerous examples of the first generation holding on to the reins.

The second generation, hence, gets the reins much later than they should and tend to delay their own Vanaprastha as well. But the importance of Vanaprastha is highly magnified for this generation as they may no longer be dealing with just siblings but also with cousins. With the increased number of people in the family, succession becomes the core issue. The onus is on them to address it. If they don't, then the seed of the curse that the third generation lives with—that they are the destroyers— is sowed by none other than the second generation.

And in the third generation, if bifurcation and efficient handover have not happened, and there are multiple owner–managers, it will result in chaos. This can have several fallouts. First: the most competent and smart one chooses to exit the chaos and hence, the business loses an able leader. Second: the same set of owner–managers creates businesses that are rivals to the existing business. Third: they start businesses that are downstream or upstream projects, putting undue pressure on the resources of the family business.

Transition literally means going from one stage to another. Vanaprastha is the transition from Grihastha to Sanyas. Out of the four stages of life, Vanaprastha, the third, is the most important and least understood. While Brahmacharya—training stage, Grihastha—transaction, and Sanyas—turn-in, are well-defined and identifiable by all, it is not only wise but mandatory to recognize Vanaprastha, the stage of transition.

From being at the helm to relinquishing leadership is tough. Most of us don't realize the onset of this stage and many remain in denial, creating uncertainties in the organization, giving wrong signals about the future of the business and encouraging unhealthy competition in the next generation. At stake is the business one has nurtured through Grihastha. A delay in succession can ruin the hard work. The transition should happen consciously while one is still in good control of the self and the organization, and should be able to navigate it peacefully and intelligently, thus engaging the organization.

Life in a family business is like a relay race. And Vanaprastha is the time to hand the baton to the next generation, just like the athletes in a 4x100 metre race do once their designated stretch of 100 metres (in the case of a family business—Grihastha) has been covered. One is programmed to hand over the baton to the next athlete so that they can continue the race. Imagine the consequences if the athlete refuses to hand over the baton or delays handing it over. The race will not be completed or will be lost. Similarly, the handing over of the business to the Chosen Family Representative (CFR) or a successor (SMB) marks the continuity of the business. A planned succession safeguards and protects the company from future calamities. Vanaprastha ensures succession and continuity and this clarity secures the family business from unnecessary manipulations and misadventures leading to succession conflicts, which have deep-rooted consequences for any organization.

Let's take a look at Figure 7. After navigating the years of Brahmacharya in gaining knowledge, and pursuing wealth for the duration of Grihastha, is the time when one enters Vanaprastha which is associated with fame. Why is this stage associated with fame, some might question. After all, not everyone is chasing fame. One can be famous by infamy too. Is that desirable? Fame and recognition with honour are the hallmarks of Vanaprastha and it's a means and not an end to transition.

The journey of a generation is well-defined. If we follow it right, we make our lives successful. For that purpose, this stage demands the manifestation of two skills:

a)   the art of giving—charity
b)   the art of self-exploration—self-fulfilment

My elder sister, Richa, is the epitome of the art of giving. I admire that quality in her. Her visits to our home are more like fun vacations for us. We are both early risers and our most precious moments together are over innumerable cups of morning tea dipped with reminisces of the past to flavours of current affairs. Discussions on our country, economy, business, family or society are backed with personal experiences, practical viewpoints, psychological understanding and philosophical underpinnings. Her ideological belief about the art of giving is, 'One only gives what one has in excess.' A positive person will give positive ideas and solutions, while a negative person will only spread negativity. If one has excess sadness in life, they will only make you sad. People who have time in abundance will be automatically available to you. If someone has accumulated wealth, they will give it back to society as philanthropy.

We see most billionaires creating foundations to fulfil this objective—Azim Premji, Narayan Murthy, The Bill and Melinda Gates Foundation and Ford Foundation. Philanthropy can take any form: some volunteer their time, while celebrities lend their name and fame towards a cause. In my case, in my Vanaprastha, I am giving the wealth of my knowledge back to society in the form of this book, *How to Thrive in a Family Business.*

In Vedic literature, Grihastha is the time to acquire (*grahan*— to create, build and accumulate wealth) and Vanaprastha is the time of giving (*tyag*—the time to give back). Since childhood, we learn to share our things, part with old toys, extend help to elders and make donations to the poor. I classify all such acts of generosity as giving away and we should continue doing this all through our life. Vanaprastha is different. It is the stage and time to give back—to society, to the community, to business and, above all, to the self too. We have earned it all here and giving back is an acknowledgement of that—an act of gratitude. In Grihastha, we accumulate for the self and a chosen few. In Vanaprastha, when you start doing something for the community or society, it has an emotional appeal for the people it touches. Donation as an act of generosity has a different connotation while charity with a sense of gratitude is humbling; it softens the mind to cede things, and brings along honour and regard. This status and state of mind makes it easy to hand over the business to a successor.

The second thing that helps in transition is the art of self-exploration. It is all about giving back to the self. Stepping away from the day-to-day management of the family business leaves a lot of time at hand. This should be utilized in doing what you love and are passionate about. Everyone has a talent, a hobby, or interest in a subject or a commitment towards a cause. Vanaprastha is where one has to fulfil their desires and latent dreams. Not for self-promotion or marketing oneself but for being the real person you are. I have seen business owners pursue politics, art or culture. I have witnessed some becoming accomplished artists and chefs, venturing into opening eateries, and acquiring an authoritative status in the chosen field. This brings respect and recognition for the self. In the hierarchy of needs, esteem is a natural progression.

Self-exploration never ends. It starts in Vanaprastha and continues through Sanyas. There is no destination; it's an ongoing search for ways of self-fulfilment.

Some are fortunate in realizing their full potential by combining their passion with philanthropy. This marks the start of self-actualization which leads one to the ultimate goal of relinquishment. Thus, Vanaprastha is also the time to get ready to embrace Sanyas. Since it is not easy to turn-in, and requires a direction for transformation of the mind and soul, Vanaprastha gives you that time to lay the groundwork.

The stage of partial retirement from business—Vanaprastha—can be better understood if one understands the purpose of the business. For some, it could be a passion; for some, a legacy to follow. For others, it could be a matter of status and recognition. Some might just be there to keep themselves busy. Whatever plausible reason one can think of, all of them are about the 'I'. You are advised to step aside a bit from this 'I' and ask yourself a question: When 'I' am not here, what is the purpose of this business? The answer will flow. And you have understood Vanaprastha. This brings us to the next sin, which is the first in Vanaprastha.

Sin 23: Not Realizing the Dawn of Vanaprastha

It is important to highlight that many of us don't know when Vanaprastha should formally start, and, more importantly, when it has actually arrived. Hence, most of us get into denial mode while we should start preparing for it.

There are no clear-cut pointers, or a defined age where you can decide that it is time to hand over the business. The duration it takes in handing over the baton is also not defined. It's very personal to every individual, and the process is unique to every family business.

The scriptures divide our lives into four ashrams, allocating twenty-five years to each stage of life for discharging our duties as expected in each ashram—from birth to twenty-five years of age should be Brahmacharya; from twenty-six to fifty Grihastha; and fifty-one to seventy-five Vanaprastha. Sanyas is the balance of life from age seventy-six onwards. Averaging out varying life expectancies, some literatures suggest each stage to be of twenty-four years, indicating the start of Vanaprastha at forty-eight. Wisdom of elders in the family business recommends that one must start planning from the time a grandchild is born. Given the marriageable age criteria that was the norm in India earlier, it suggests that Vanaprastha starts anywhere between forty and forty-five years of age. I have seen families that are ready for succession when a successor is available. Such fixed doctrines can sometimes become a wasp trap.

I suggest a more structured methodology to figure out when Vanaprastha has arrived. We need to see it from the angle of all the stakeholders in this situation. There are three stakeholders who are relevant at the time of Vanaprastha. First is the business itself; second, the generation receiving the business; and the third is the generation handing over the business.

Timely realization of the dawn of Vanaprastha and then looking for a meritorious solution are the key takeaways of Sin 23. Hence, seeing it from all three perspectives, we may ask these questions to decide if Vanaprastha has arrived for you:

1. Is the business stagnating?

When the business starts to slow down and there is a decline in business revenue, it is a clear indication that your input to the business is not effective any more. In a way, you are causing it to stagnate. People confuse stagnation and decline as different concepts. They feel that if you are stagnant, then it's still positive as '. . . at least, you are not declining. I am the same as I was last year.' But stagnation means decline. Considering time and value of money with inflation, if you aren't growing, you're declining. There can be several reasons for it, but from the perspective of the business, there is a need for change in leadership. It might be because you are not exposed to newer technologies or opportunities; or maybe with advancement in age, you are being conservative and not experimenting or expanding as much. It is time to face reality—if the business is getting stagnant, it is definitely time for the handover of the management.

2. Are you facing health issues?

As we age, our body and mind become more and more susceptible to ailments, sometimes leading to disabilities too. With our lifestyle choices, as we grow older, the risk of chronic diseases also increases. Midlife is when genetic health issues also crop up. Most of us are proactive and look after our health to maintain a healthy work-life balance and even beyond. But when the time spent on managing health issues starts to eat into work time, it is an indication that it is time to step out and discharge yourself from the duties of the management, and put in place an effective successor.

Poor health of the working owner can have multiple fallouts on the business as their own productivity starts to drop. This has a ripple effect within the enterprise. Disability of the owner sometimes creates an atmosphere of an old-age home in the office space—sombre and lethargic instead of dynamic and energetic. Young employees can start to show signs of diminishing morale. In the case of public limited companies, their reputation and share prices take a hit. Staff may start taking advantage of the owner's absenteeism, thus disturbing the work culture of the organization. It's only healthy to realize that Vanaprastha has arrived.

3. Do you have a successor ready in the next generation?

If the answer is yes, you are a fortunate owner who has a competent, ready-to-move-in successor. How many parents have capable sons or daughters who can take up the responsibility of the business? You have probably managed the Brahmacharya of your child right. And this places you in an ideal setting to start the handover process and live your Vanaprastha right.

There are many families who have not nurtured their children through their Brahmacharya, leaving them inadequately skilled. It is such families who just assume that the next generation is ready because they have graduated and entered the business. Mere presence in business is no indication of abilities; but families wrongly presume that the business will, from then on, be the next generation's responsibility and their hard work will determine their destiny while the family has nothing to do with it.

Many families believe in simply handing over and letting the next generation run the business the way they want to without checking if they were ready for it. It will be disastrous to have the successor have their way while you consider it to be their destiny—an area that you cannot see or control. But the fact is that destiny is a culmination of our choices. It is imperative to distinguish between a ready-to-manage successor and an available next generation.

4. Is there no heir for the business?

There are situations when none of the successors are willing to continue with the business. They may want to pursue their own passion. Sometimes, values come in the way as the next generation does not want to pursue a certain line of business. The next generation may not want to get into fields of business such as tobacco or alcohol due to their perceived righteousness. Jewellery is a business which, at times, gives some a liability nightmare. Then there are also times when the successor is aware of their inability to make a particular type of business succeed or feels under-skilled for it. Classic examples are export–import businesses, or ones which are heavy on interpersonal skills such as liaison. What if there are no heirs in the family?

All the above situations are a clear indication of the arrival of Vanaprastha and from the perspective of the business, it demands a plan for its continuity and survival. In such circumstances, it is best to find a suitor who can buy the business. Most owners try to sell off the business in their Sanyas stage. It is advisable to do so during Vanaprastha when you are in control of the self and the business which will help you get the right market valuation.

5. Are you bored and are avoiding the workplace?

Entrepreneurs and business leaders need a strong motivation to lead their business. It is observed that over a period of time, the business stops motivating them. You may not feel the exhilaration of a challenge in the way it did when you started. In all probability, over time, you have mastered your role to such an extent that it has become a way of life. This routine starts to bog you down and creates boredom. Many of us need obstacles to keep us challenged. We need to be the firefighters of the organization to feel a sense of self-worth.

As organizations expand, younger employees are hired. This team brings in younger ideas and a dynamic work environment. This can be very unnerving and discomfiting for some in their midlife, causing them to start avoiding the workplace.

Businesses grow and cross a threshold from where a new set of skills is required to manage it. Some business owners feel the heat as the challenges are beyond their own skills. Consequently, their interest starts waning since they have little to contribute. It is time to pursue your passion outside of the business and step back and leave it in the hands of someone who is better skilled and proficient at handling the expanding business.

6. Are you secure enough to hand over the management?

Securing yourself financially and emotionally before handing over the business is important for the benefit of your own self. You are handing over the money-making machinery that you used to control completely. So, how do you ensure that you won't be dependent on the support of your children?

There are many ways to keep this security, depending on the situation and the respective families. You might hand over management of the business, but keep ownership. With this ownership, you will keep receiving your share of profits. Or you could keep the assets and create a money-generating mechanism through them.

One might wonder what one would do with this money. While medical expenses are a biggie, they are not the only spending spots. You are handing over the business, not ending your life. Rather, you are entering a different phase of life where you have to give back to yourself by pursuing your passion or give back to society by way of philanthropy and charity. This helps with the continuity of appreciation and importance that you enjoyed while you were running a business. You still feel important and appreciated, which remains a cornerstone of this phase.

Sin 24: Not Being Ready to Let Go or Reluctance in Handing Over the Management

If you are handing over the management, you need to ask yourself if you are ready to let it go. And if you are not willing to let it go to a ready-to-take next generation, then you need to start preparing for it.

History is witness to kingdoms grooming their future king under the watchful eyes of the present one, who is an integral part of this shaping-up exercise for an impending transition.

However, when the time is right, most get cold feet. They look at ways to prolong their own tenure. Why only history? We see this happening a lot among royalty even today. The transfer of power happens through coronation and there is no room and, literally speaking, no palace for the outgoing king or queen. We are witness to this phenomenon of holding back and not handing over the reins in all aspects of life, be it the corporate world, political organizations, the judiciary or the bureaucracy.

It is seen that at times, the lifestyle and rituals of business families get wrongly inspired by royalty. Some families get impressed by the rituals and grandeur of the coronation ceremony and replicate this idea in their family business. But the situation here is very different. The concept of Vanaprastha and the analogy of the ashrams have been introduced to make the process of transition spread over a period of time, making it systematic and non-traumatic. Transition in business cannot be a light switch that you can turn on or off any time you wish. The owner cannot be a use-and-throw commodity. We are dealing with humans and looking at a win-win-win situation for all three stakeholders—the generation handing over, the generation receiving the business, and the business itself.

Not letting go is a condition which is less physical and more to do with the limbic section of the brain. The human brain has a logical section called the neocortex and an emotional section—the limbic brain. This feeling of holding on and not letting go comes from the emotional brain, making it difficult to detach and dissociate. While on the other hand, the logical brain is clear that one has to hand over and exit. This is scientific and, to explain it simply, the logical brain knows that the attachment is detrimental and communicates the same. But the emotional one needs that attachment to satisfy itself. They act as per their inherent characteristics. In the event that the business has been the best thing you ever had or the only thing, the grip tightens when you are supposed to let it go. To loosen this grip, one has to pursue the art of giving and self-fulfilment. We have already discussed the benefits in detail earlier.

Vanaprastha gives you enough time to evaluate the successor's capacities and capabilities and to assure yourself that they can take business decisions on their own. When I entered the business, I started taking my own decisions, and my father encouraged me. But he was not ready to give up as he had no alternate plans for himself. When he entered the business, my grandfather passed away. As per the charter, he took over the reins of the vertical independently and thus reflected all the first-generation behavioural patterns. He was hard-working, emotionally attached to the brand and used to micromanaging the business. Thus, the whole organizational culture became an extension of his own personality. It was difficult for him to detach from himself.

Given my skills, it was easy to adapt, work and modify the culture, but I was not handed over the management completely. My father was still in the system and had decision-making powers. I had moved to Delhi, executing the strategy laid out by him. Occasionally, I would see him questioning the same strategy which was his master plan. I realized that the relationship between a successor and whom they hope to replace is heavily charged with emotions. I can understand it better today when I am in my Vanaprastha and watching the same emotions playing out between my son—the successor—and me. With the advancement of age, you start becoming more emotional, and take decisions emotionally. Hence, if you are still in the system and not letting go, these emotion-driven decisions can hamper the business and the family. And this is exactly what happened in our case.

It was easy to influence my father—both from the business as well as family point of view. The closure of the establishment at Allahabad would affect the livelihood of a lot of employees. Many of the senior managers, along with family, convinced my father not to shut down the plant there to shift manufacturing completely to the Greater Noida plant. They argued that the

Allahabad plant was the symbol of my father's existence since he lived there. He would have no identity if this plant was closed! They played with his emotions and my father was trapped.

His friend of fifty years, Uncle Nagpal, came to condole his passing away and was reminiscing about a pact that he had made with my father. 'Ram made me build a house near his own in Delhi so that in the latter part of our lives, the two of us could give each other company as neighbours. Despite his keenness, he could never move to Delhi. My loss!'

Death is inevitable. It can come any time and Vanaprastha is the stage of life in which it should be planned for. By now, the future and current resources are in place. Wealth accumulation in Grihastha is at your disposal. One of the life partners will ultimately be survived by the other. This uncertainty could be anyone's guess, but the plan should cover both eventualities. In India, we follow a norm of maintaining an age difference between a husband and a wife. Sometimes, the male is five to seven years older than his wife. Thus, the chances of the male leaving a widow behind are higher. If the male is the sole breadwinner of the family, it is imperative to plan for the financial security of the spouse who might face two key problems in her widowhood— economic constraints and neglect. Making suitable plans to take care of both is advised. Family businesses provide platforms in the form of family office, trusts and philanthropy organizations for this very purpose. One can maintain economic independence and also avoid feeling marginalized or lonely.

As these decisions are important and difficult to take, one definitely needs support to arrive at favourable conclusions. It becomes important to identify who you can fall back upon, or take advice from. A true adviser will always keep the end goal in mind while offering advice. Decisions should be essayed out in writing, preferably in the form of a will. This act removes reluctance and prepares the mind to let go. I particularly like to quote from the Mahabharata, where Duryodhana sought the advice of his uncle, Shakuni, who made him take decisions that eventually led to the war of the Mahabharata. On the other hand, Arjun had Krishna to guide and advise him, thus making him the great warrior he became.

To conclude, while planning the handover, one needs good advice and a passion for self-fulfilment to overcome this emotional sin.

Sin 25: Not Moving Towards Professionalization in the Third Generation

'You have been given the reins of the business. And it is your responsibility to successfully hand it over to the next generation. Since you didn't start the business, you have no right to shut it.'

These words by my uncle from Nagpur keep reverberating in my head. I am the third generation—the one that decides whether the family business will proudly contribute to the increase in the statistical figure of 20 per cent survival, or if it will be relegated to the ranks of the 80 per cent has-beens. Words carry weight and their burden has been heavy for me. I have known, since childhood, the responsibilities of my generation. He was expecting something out of me and, well, words do have the power to move mountains.

In instances where early division has not taken place or a consensus candidate is not operating the business as a CFR, while there are multiple members working in the business, then the third generation has no other option but to become owners and stop aspiring to be managers. Why do owners aspire to become managers in the first place? Because recognition is linked to founders of the business who were owner–managers. Because there is pressure from society and you need to validate yourself, thus restricting your thoughts and vision to your own personal self and not extending them to the overall benefit of the business. I am not ashamed to mention that my son, a fourth generation, within a short period of working within the organization, keeps telling my generation to stop behaving like managers and act like owners.

Further, the skill of micromanagement, a boon for a first-generation businessman, can become counter-productive for the third generation. By the third generation, most businesses are at a sizeable scale of operations, with a well-functioning organizational structure in place as compared to what the business may have been in an earlier generation.

As a part of a crisis management plan, it becomes mandatory to bifurcate ownership and management. If one has to get out of management, you have no other option but to bring in professionals to manage the business, consultants to provide you with the skills to manage the managers and a charter to manage the family. It is ideal that the second generation does it. But in case it didn't happen then, the onus is on the third generation or else, they should be prepared for the consequences.

Most members do not possess the skills required for this transformation and even if they make an effort, not many in the workplace environment actually are in favour. It could be a family member or senior managers who look at opportunities to scuttle the process. What better than orchestrating hiring a wrong team. This poses a challenge as hiring is a specialized and tricky process. After all, professionals are not the ones with a magic wand. Bringing them in is primarily to establish boundaries in the workplace, which do not exist between family members. With family in the management, one cannot separate business from personal, leading to conflicts. Help should be sought for executing this hiring exercise. The professional team has to contribute to growth, otherwise, the whole exercise becomes counterproductive.

When we decided to professionalize our vertical, the first obstacle was the budget for hiring. The family agreed to go ahead, but in the cheapest way possible. No one wanted to reduce their take-home and reinvest it. Or was that a way to ensure that it did not go through? I am not sure but our first attempt was a failure. This had varying impact on the people already working with us. One could see relief on some faces, while some were relieved about the fact that we washed our hands off a wrong team early on, before they caused tremendous harm. The ones opposing the move hoped that the failure might discourage us owners from attempting a similar move in the future. They were in favour of maintaining the status quo. Some started approaching the family with their own views to influence our minds, for not professionalizing. Some exited the organization because they knew that professionalization was inevitable and they could not envisage themselves in the organizational chart once that had happened.

In our vertical, the fourth generation had already begun work and more members were on the threshold of entering the business. My siblings and I were beginning to get edgy; we wanted a solution. Time was running out and we, the third generation, had no other option but to think seriously about how to make the move from a family business to the idea of being a business family; professionalize and convert the business into a corporate enterprise; consolidate ownership and hand the management over to the CXO team. Our need was transforming into desperation.

The first debacle had taught us a lot, especially the difference between hiring a manager and hiring a true professional to carry out management. In common parlance, we treat all senior management folks as professionals but these are misguided perceptions. Our budget constraints did not allow us access to a skilled pool of the right professionals and I did not want to repeat the mistake of hiring non-professional managers. True to the adage—if you offer peanuts, you will get monkeys—we did not want to waste money, but we also needed the turnaround.

They say, 'When one reaches out desperately for something, the universe responds.' We found an opportunity to combine the verticals of Baidyanath. We could pool in our talents and resources and move towards professionalization. Most importantly, we got budgets to hire people who were not restricted to a mindset of only serving themselves but also the business. We needed a team for whom Baidyanath was a challenging opportunity and not just another job. It had to bring them accolades in the circles that mattered to them.

Is a professional really different? Yes, a professional is different from an average vocation seeker. They are responsible and answerable to their job. Accountability comes with freedom to operate the business. They are not married to the business; instead, they are there to do a job. They must feel challenged and motivated at what they do or else they will move on before the designated period. Their compensation is based on results. Therefore, time is of the essence. So, decision-making and solution-providing become priorities. They must be masters of deliberate choices and cognitive thinking. They survive because of their skills. Hence, they constantly upgrade themselves in terms of skills to be masters in their respective field of operation. They follow their own career path and do not resort to sycophancy, manoeuvring, or playing up to promoters. Owners must ensure that the professional is ethical towards job responsibilities and has high moral standards.

On a lighter note, political parties sometimes behave like business entities or display all traits of a family business. If such is the case, they should stop seeking self-validation and corporatize the structure for mass appeal and continuity. Most political parties fail because of family feuds and members not following the ashrams of life, especially Vanaprastha, the stage where succession is to be implemented. Indian political parties and (some) family businesses are prepared to go down instead of having a more competent person operate the show. Passing on the reins is not the simplest decision to make; it has its cons too, but by the third generation, it becomes a TINA (There Is No Alternative) factor. Can the family run their own business? Do they really have to depend on outsiders? They can, if they have the required skills and all members agree.

But the problem starts when owner–managers replicate past generation successes and micromanage the business. They face difficult situations themselves and hence, are ever-willing to justify an unsatisfactory result. Some also become soft towards their managers, overlooking their below-par performance to compensate for their own weaknesses. Complacency sets in. Some families induct members in the business based on just one qualification—they belong to the family. Such owner–managers are under-skilled for the role. They chase unrealistic goals, resulting in failure. Regular failures demoralize any organization. People leave or just do routine jobs in a mechanical way, missing out on actual opportunities. Whereas a good manager is one who has the appetite to take chances as well as calculated risks.

There are working family members who are good at certain jobs. They get so steeped in the process of managing, that results become secondary. They are always eager to highlight the process and are constantly training juniors; precious time that must be used for evaluating results is spent on discussing the process. Non-performing employees under them get into the habit of highlighting the difficulties of the process to hide their non-achievements while the achievers brag about difficulties to enhance their own importance in front of seniors. People are appreciated and even promoted because of the gift of the gab.

It is not always family infighting that destroys the business; incompetence of working members plays a bigger role in the closure of many family businesses. Take for example, a business which is in its third generation. It would typically be between sixty and 100 years old. It has survived for so many years because of its strengths and successes in the industry it operates in. Success attracts competition. Multiple competitors make forays into that product category, starting a war to attract customers. I choose the word war to get across my point that wars are not fought single-handedly or with bare hands. One has to have a team of highly-skilled people to remain ahead in business.

Some third generations also start parenting the business. Families must stop treating their business like their children, especially those who find it difficult to come to terms with the fact that the business has grown from adolescence to adulthood. Businesses like an offspring are dependent on their creator who must devote time 24x7—in effect, micromanage the baby. Imagine using the same kid gloves in adulthood; we all know the consequences—'Either the business will leave you, or you will never let it grow up!' The scale any business acquires by the third generation requires a different set of techniques to operate and such talent should be sourced from outside.

You need commando-like professionals, each displaying their own skill and strength. Today, successors are likely to be armed with better education and skill-sets than their predecessors, but that is not reason enough for them to lead the mature third-generation business. Such successors must take informed decisions, they should carry out a diagnosis of the marketplace, business environment and competitors as these keep changing with time. Given the global scenario, competition must be studied carefully. Business strengths and counter-strategies must match. A successful CFR is the one who builds a competent team of professionals to lead the business, and is also able to dodge the pressure of accommodating family members in the management who are seeking to hide their unsuccessful careers and incompetencies.

Families that have multiple members working in a business face their own challenges. Why do family businesses have multiple working members? It has a lot to do with succession planning or having a weak family head. Some families decide to give work opportunities to all its members, and, at times, there is interference from non-working family members because of issues related to PRIME. Most of them may just be mere representatives of different branches of the family tree, not because they have the skills or the leadership qualities the business requires. They all have ownership and carry their own agenda.

The one hankering for appreciation will take credit for work done by managers, while another may demand attention and respect from employees for his dwindling self-esteem. There are some wanting popularity and will go around helping employees and being over-friendly to them, thus disrupting the discipline in the company, while some are genuinely benevolent. You are likely to spot a family member with the biggest office, equipped with the latest gadgets that look hardly used. Such personalities call for meetings in their swanky offices to put up photos on social media and head off for the golf course. There are some who want all the authority but shy away from responsibility. They have their own set of values that are detrimental to the organization and their day is spent in social engagements or page-three events.

The ones with a big ego will create 'Yes' men in the organization, playing favourites to retain them. Favouritism takes centre stage and sibling egos clash, personal bias creeps in while evaluating the performance of managers, and so on. These actions make the organization unproductive and incompetent to survive in a competitive marketplace. Professionalization can ensure that all members keep enjoying their agendas without disturbing management or the business.

Some owners in the third generation, with a sense of commitment, do take the lead but can get demotivated along the way, attributing the unhealthy environment to their own personal failure. Sometimes, panic sets in and owners step in with half-baked solutions. Such influences of owner–managers are detrimental for the business. Family members start hiding their incompetence in the name of infighting. Instead of looking for a viable solution, a blame-game starts. Suggestions start pouring in from all directions—right from finding a suitor to getting a part owner. The ones with their own agenda suffer from myopia, and are unable to come up with sustainable solutions. This is the time for the third generation to act; to open the third eye—the eye of wisdom. Will Mahesh destroy the business, or destroy the wrong practices of the family business?

I am Mahesh, the third generation who must orchestrate disruption in business; not its destruction. This is the true role of the third generation. It's time they reorganize the family and restructure the business to make it relevant for the third generation. Supported by ideologically similar third-generation members, we at Baidyanath have embarked on our journey to destroy wrong practices; one better understands it as the disruption of the working style. If every third generation can face this reality and work towards breaking the curse, the new norm will be something like this: the first generation creates, the second manages and the third disrupts—to create a new order. This is the ideal cycle for any successful family business.

When some families cannot see eye to eye and cannot plan a future together, it is better to find a suitor from outside, but it is not advisable to find an investing owner. You do have the option of giving someone part ownership. As soon as you do that, the family business doesn't remain a family business any more and this will upset the shareholding cart. In fact, even in our family, we had an offer where the proposer would become the CEO and own 2 per cent of the company. He stated that he knew how this business worked since he had closely worked in a similar business and had domain knowledge. But the family was apprehensive and did not consider the proposal for similar reasons.

Zandu Pharmaceuticals was owned by two families—one of them exited by giving up their shareholding in favour of Emami Limited. This could have upset the balance of ownership and management, causing the second family's exit as well. So, you either sell off the business completely or learn to own and manage it as a family. It is advisable to sell a running business and get a full valuation for it. Experimenting with any of the middle paths can ultimately risk loss of ownership and potential loss of wealth at all levels.

Whether you are the successor, or a CFR, treat your role as a stop-gap arrangement, because, in the long run, the family business will survive only if you professionalize and exit from management. This sin should not be committed for the sake of continuity. To move away from a method-appreciative organization to a result-oriented one is what I define as professionalization of the organization.

Now the question is—what remains of your own role in the business when you want to professionalize it? There is a bigger role awaiting you: managing the management. One thing that's largely misunderstood is that there is no work when it comes to just ownership. From personal experience I can say that the responsibilities, in fact, increase. One can get out of the comfort zone of day-to-day management, but taking over a completely new governance process that needs to be monitored continuously has its challenges. While at the management level, the game may have been that of snakes and ladders, as owners, it becomes a game of chess—the game of strategy and mind. The reality is that a lot of family members are insecure about moving out of the management as they don't have the know-how to play the new game. This takes us to the next sin.

Sin 26: Letting the Circles Completely Overlap or Be Mutually Exclusive

Remember the circles I drew on a tissue paper at the wedding? The two circles and the right overlap are the elixir of a family business. While you have understood that set A and set B cannot overlap completely as that is an assured disaster, we do commit a sin if we don't ensure that it doesn't happen the other way around, i.e., the two sets have absolutely no overlap with each other and are mutually exclusive.

Figure 8

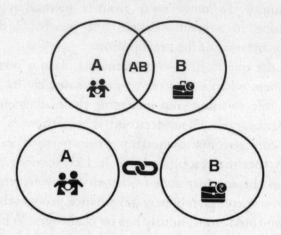

Where:
AB = Family managing/governing the business
A = Family
B = Business
A and B must be connected by management or governance.
They should not move apart.

To understand it better, let's take a look at a classic scenario:
Family businesses in their first generation have an ideal
overlap of set A and B. This is so because of the presence of
the creator–manager. In the second generation, the business is
in the hands of a family–owner–manager. The area of overlap
starts to change depending on the number of members entering
the management and variations begin to emerge. By the third
generation, it is the shareholder–manager who is at the helm.
The chances of the two sets completely overlapping or moving
away from each other is the highest. Once again, the buck stops
at the third generation. Typically, it happens in the third but, in
reality, it can happen in any generation including the first. Why
do the sets move away from each other?

The first generation starts the journey of the business full of passion and by micromanaging it. They are good executors of plans and are governed by self—the entrepreneur. The role is clear and the road ahead may not be smooth, but it is straight. The separation of the business from the owner in the first generation is more for personal reasons and has their consent. They are the creators and has complete rights to take a decision. Hence, it does not get covered as a sin in this context. Let's understand what happens to the businesses that move into the next generation.

When the second generation embarks on their journey, there appears a fork in the road—a junction where choices have to be made as to which direction to move in, what route to finalize. One arrow indicates management and the other governance. The choice the second generation makes is crucial as it alters the future of any family business. Most choose to get into day-to-day management and hire a battery of professionals—CAs, consultants, tax experts and lawyers—for governance. These specialists assist and manage an area where the government governs the business and cannot be equated with the governance of the business as an owner. The owners' is a role that cannot be left vacant, especially without an operative family charter. Some families mandate that some members look after day-to-day affairs and others govern it, laying the ground for ownership conflicts. Effectively, the choice has to be made and it's only wise that they should choose to govern the business, professionalize the organization and start managing the management, thus behaving like perfect owners.

Taking the road to governance maintains the overlap balance of the sets. But lack of good systems and MIS, governance of business and lack of checks on the professional team can sometimes make the two sets exclusive of each other. A similar situation can arise in the third generation. The introduction of a team of professionals is as necessary for them as managing and controlling them. By and large, one hires a team which is smarter than the owners, so that it can ensure good company performance.

These very people, once they get to know the business well, can misuse their power and authority. Keeping a check is being safe than sorry, and it also ensures a healthy overlap of sets.

This can turn into a disadvantage of professionalization, especially if dishonesty creeps in—cases of negligence and fraud begin to plague an organization. There could be attempts to separate sets A and B. The possibility of a takeover by the professionals should never arise. The owner cannot be made irrelevant. Family control and status of a family business should never be compromised. The family must make a clear and effective transition from day-to-day management of the business to governing the business and managing the professionals, who have the means to separate the two circles.

The series of board games at Infosys, which the media covered widely, is the right eye-opener for this sin. So, the overlap must be of the owners displaying effective governance practices to ensure that the boards managing the business do not edge out the family. The two circles must not separate, making one lose their inheritance.

Figure 9

So, in the first generation,
balance is maintained by a management overlap.
Sets A and B overlap, where AB = Management

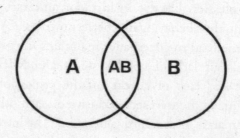

Figure 10

By the third generation, it must be a governance overlap:

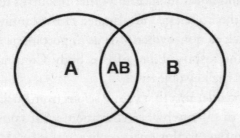

Sets A and B overlap, where AB = Governance

What is the difference between management and governance? Management has to ensure smooth functioning for the growth of the business, as visualized and formalized by the governing body. Governance is setting goals and providing resources for the business to flourish within the policies and procedures laid out by the body. The word governance is derived from 'govern', which means to keep in check. Corporate governance is about controlling executives and protecting and preserving the rights of the shareholders, while executive management effectively works towards optimizing earnings for shareholders. There are opinions that management and governance both manage the business, and hence, there is not much of a difference between the two. What sets them apart is that they manage at different levels. In fact, management and governance have to stay within these well-defined boundaries and should not digress from their respective roles for the smooth running of the business. Another differentiator is that the onus of hiring the CXO team, which manages the business, is on the governing body and not vice versa. Governance also creates the mission statement for the organization.

In a family business, governance is essentially representative of the owner–family. The governing body can consist of the whole family or, at times, the family collectively hires a group of non-family members proficient in their roles to govern the CXO team as representatives of the family, or it can be a combination of both. They define the vision and create a roadmap; appoint the A team and inject finance and other resources to achieve the set goals of the business. Governance of the family too—both owners as well as non-owners—is as important as the business and is also the responsibility of this body. Continuity of both sets becomes the key objective.

A common dilemma that young scions from business families face: I want to pursue higher education; what course should I study? The answer to this question lies in this sin. Is your family managing the day-to-day business, or is it already into the governing stage? Is it currently in management but do you want to take it into governance? The course you want to pursue should contribute towards helping you develop skills that you will need for the future you who will be leading the business.

While family businesses are similar to each other, what makes them unique is the size of sets A and B. In reality, both the sets do not increase or decrease in size simultaneously and are never proportionate to each other. It is all a numbers game. This creates situations where there are complete overlaps—set A over B or B over A. The size of set A is determined by the number of family members and the business's revenue numbers decide the size of set B.

Without a proper governance mechanism in place, the two sets get into a tussle for stability and functionality for themselves, leading to the need to control the other. If the family number increases and overshadows business numbers, it behaves like a mother kangaroo carrying the business around in her pouch. On the other hand, if the business becomes too large and the family set remains small, the business eclipses the owner–family to become an entity by itself. Both these situations must be avoided through proper governance practices.

Based on the generation the business is in, governance mechanisms vary drastically. From the Victorian mindsets of earlier generations, it moves towards more democratic governance practices. Family dynamics of siblings and cousins mixed with intergenerational complexities make the balancing of interests of individual owners and the growth trajectory of the business unique to every family. A cohesive joint front is needed to govern. The need to earn an income for the family that was dominant in earlier generations converts into a desire for wealth appreciation by shareholding owners.

The emergence of the owner–family and their needs requires us to look at the more-evolved structure as seen in the three-set model in Figure 11. Once the family business reaches this stage, governance has to balance the dynamics of behavioural patterns emerging from all three different sets. It helps if each set has a common agenda and response to the business. It reduces the fear of one set overshadowing the other drastically, which is easier in a two-set environment. Thus, it also eliminates the chances of two sets completely overlapping each other or the sets becoming mutually exclusive.

Figure 11

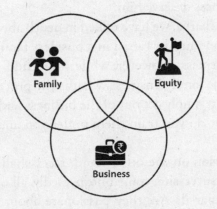

Good governance practices maintain a healthy area of overlap. In larger families, they give a voice to every member and make them operate as a team towards achieving a shared goal or planning a joint future. Governance builds trust and members feel secure from the threat of being maliciously edged out of ownership and its benefits. In order to secure family business heritage and to avoid this sin, a robust governance system must be in place.

Sin 27: Not Having a Succession Plan

'If a family intends the business to remain in family hands, succession must be considered a process, not an endpoint.'
—Peter Englisch, EY Global and EMEIA Family Business Leader

Succession of the business can be an exciting but also a tricky experience. You are basically giving away your legacy and hard work of several years. While you are elated that the next generation is taking over, you are also anxious about how it will pan out. Am I handing it over to the right person? Will the successor be able to deliver? Is he deserving of the business, or does the business deserve him?

In Brahmacharya, we have talked in depth about the way the next generation must be raised in a business family in favour of the family business. However, while your child is ready to be inducted in the family business, what is the process of handing it over? Do you simply get out of the business and let them take your place? Or do you train them under you and then hand it over?

The successor, on the other hand, faces challenges of their own. Did the succession come unexpectedly, all of a sudden, or were they prepared? Are they passionate about the business? How do employees and other stakeholders perceive them? Will they continue or leave the organization? Is the family satisfied with the choice or is there resentment regarding the candidature?

Is this the business I really want for the rest of my life? Should I keep it or sell it?

Contrary to what appears to be simple and linear, the handing over of business is a complex process and must be approached with extreme caution, precision and thorough understanding of stakeholders. When you are planning to hand over a business, you have to look at many hidden layers. What helps here is a clear-cut succession plan which answers multiple questions discreetly.

For example,

1. Who will enter?
2. How will they enter?
3. When will they enter?
4. What attributes need to be considered for entry?
5. What must be made mandatory: a basic educational qualification or an interview?
6. Does his mindset go with the business and the brand?
7. Does he possess the talent and skills?
8. How can the transformation be executed?

These may look like a set of random questions, but they are actually the most critical ones. Ayurveda has taught me that the cure of complex ailments is hidden in simple things in nature.

An effective succession plan has to be unique to the family business and must be well-thought-out, as per the nature and history of the business itself. Family values, business strategy and the owners' vision can be achieved by first answering these questions to arrive at a workable plan.

Why are people reluctant to plan? The similarities between families and their individual distinctions reflect in the way they approach their arguments for not planning. I am going to share some that may sound familiar and some that I find bizarre. Some of these situations may actually exist and some may not, but it does provide reason enough to stay at the helm longer. The most common reason I have encountered is when family heads feel that they still have unfulfilled goals to meet. The 'I' and 'my dreams' cannot perceive anything beyond that. There are some who set milestones like the turnover of the company or the global expansion of the business. These individuals are rigid about the fact that they will consider succession only after these milestones are achieved. Sometimes, these are unrealistic targets that can hamper succession planning. For sure, there are delays.

The most unpleasant excuse of them all is the need to build a strong team to manage the business. Family heads believe that a prosperous business keeps the family happy. Hence, their time is devoted towards this future planning. What about succession? Well, in this case, the idea is to make the family irrelevant and dependent on loyal senior management. In such cases, the family head is actually building a team for himself for his Vanaprastha and Sanyas. He shrouds his act as professionalization; thus it cannot be passed as a succession plan. Such family–owners do not plan for what happens after them and it cannot be classified as a succession plan.

Some owners are uneasy about sharing space with a future successor as organizations have a tendency to gravitate towards the future leader. So, they might have identified the successor, but do not disclose it. Another common reason is the fear of the change that the new successor will bring. Undoing of the legacy and of existing systems and processes makes them feel that their own work is being repudiated.

Most cannot deal with the loss of authority. Hence, they keep delaying succession. Some want the respect and attention of all their children while they are alive. Therefore, they don't announce a successor, their justification being that they love all their children equally and don't want any child to feel wronged. Such a patriarch is scared to face the resentment of his children once succession is planned. They avoid problems in their lifetime. They are willing to leave the conflict of succession because of their weak character.

Problems of succession are a common occurrence in family businesses. Experienced family groups too face succession pangs. The Birla family experienced it in the 1980s, while the

Tata Group went through it quite recently. Given the structure of our family, in our second generation, there was a complete disconnect between succession in management and inheritance of ownership. The wiser third generation has sensibly sorted out this ambiguity to a large extent. Succession planning cannot be brushed under the carpet for fear of problems arising in execution.

The succession plan must be detailed enough to provide solutions to the problems that may not have occurred yet, but are possible. One has to ensure that conflicts are not passed on to the next generation. While we reflected on our own succession and respective failures, along with those of others, the following key points will help one arrive at a healthy succession plan:

A) Successor versus CFR

Most families have a ready-to-move-in successor. In all probability, there is only one family member who took to the family business and demonstrated the requisite skills to lead it. If not, then conduct an exercise within the family to find the right fit. They will be the CFR designated to manage the business on behalf of others, who will remain pure owners. A CFR can be a family or non-family member. While all successors get their respective share of the earnings and can multiply the money with the time available with them, the chosen successor—if a family member—is actually working for other successors and losing the opportunity to multiply their own money. Hence, it is pure wisdom to suitably reward the chosen successor for taking up the responsibility.

B) Elder vs competent

The 3C criteria is the most popular tool for succession planning. Selection based on character, competence and communication skills identifies the best candidate for the business. We have discussed the merits and demerits of the elder son syndrome in Sin 1. If the family follows the tradition of the eldest being the successor, then it becomes customary to hand over the business to the eldest son. The process of planning does not exist in such cases which may deprive the business of a meritorious candidate.

Succession by age could also be by default. The eldest starts working with the father while the other siblings are still in school. The father trains him and feels his job is over. With advancing age, he may not want to put in the same effort to train the others. The eldest becomes a successor by default and is more of a figurehead and not the most competent one, as the family is not aware of the capabilities of the other siblings. They could be far superior in skills for the business. Hence, this should be replaced by modern techniques available for choosing a successor and ensuring business growth. The 3C criteria is a must for succession planning. Selection that is not based on character, competence and communication skills is unlikely to grow the business, leading to sibling conflicts.

C) Giving it to someone who doesn't share the vision with the business and family

Let's say there are two possible successors—both having the right kind of skills and training for the business. But at the same time, it is not guaranteed that they will also have the same vision for the business and the family. Hence, the one who shares the vision for the business with the family and feels for the growth of the family should be given preference in the choice for succession.

D) The financial security of the family

While the vision is important, what's more critical is ensuring the financial security of the family. It cannot be disturbed. The chosen successor has to maintain balance, i.e., he cannot compromise on the growth of the business due to family pressure. And at the same time, he cannot compromise on the income of the family, even if the business demands it. This balance is a must. Sometimes, the family might be at a crossroads, whereby, if they get used to a certain amount of income, it gets difficult for them to give it up while the business may require a fresh infusion of capital for growth.

E) Emotion influences decisions

Choosing a successor has to be devoid of emotions. There is jealousy between siblings; rivalry between cousins, and grudges among them over past issues that could lead to an error in identifying the right successor. A family, after all, is made up of mortal human beings. Humans are humans because they have emotions. Negative emotions can tear apart the very fabric of rationale by making one take bad decisions. Companies are bound to fail if the family emotions arising out of conflicts drives the change. Emotions and moods make us react to the same situation differently. Hence, decisions should not be taken instantaneously but after careful thought. The decision of identifying a successor should never be taken single-handedly. This will shield that crucial decision from emotions coming in the way of deciding a suitable successor.

In fact, I have personally seen generations that are responsible for the decision, not selecting the best successor as he may outshine the previous generation, which is too much to handle for their own egos.

F) Letting one person monopolize the family business

I won't say a family business is exactly a democracy. It is difficult to bind it in the existing nomenclature of the political system. But it is not a dictatorship either. It has been experienced that there is at least one person in the entire history of the family business who has tried to grab hold of the entire business to become Aurangzeb. The person's ambition overgrows—there can be several reasons for it—and this particular member might try to overthrow everyone else to take hold of all the power and become a self-appointed successor.

Even if this person has skills that are better than anyone else's, he will still not be the right person to succeed because the family at large is linked to the business. If one person takes complete control, there is a high risk that the business will not take care of the entire family as time progresses. It must be duly addressed by the charter of the family, otherwise, it can even result in family disputes that are bound to go public and end up in courts, leading to the shutting down of the business or it being sold out at a price that is well below market valuation.

G) Gender-neutral

Women in the family are increasingly expressing interest in joining the family business. They are being encouraged to do so as well. This is an excellent opportunity as it creates a sense of belonging, and in turn builds trust. Today, education and exposure have created capable women entrepreneurs like Nisa Godrej and the Reddy sisters at Apollo, to name a few. Gender bias should now be thrown out of the window and considered a thing of the past.

Having said that, families do have clauses in their charter where they do not include the girl child or the wife of the owner. It can be a conscious decision for reasons best known to the family, but it should not be out of a bias. Maintaining gender parity gives a business a bigger pool of candidates to choose from and provides answers where there are none.

'I was very fortunate—my father, my mentor, did not differentiate between his son and daughter. I never felt that I was any different. I didn't have to fight for my position in the organization; I had to demonstrate that I deserved it.'

—Vinita Gupta, CEO,
Lupin Ltd. and Lupin Pharmaceuticals, Inc.

H) Communicate the decision of the successor

When people don't have clear communication, it leads to misinterpretation. Inheritors start interpreting according to their own logic and convenience. Later, this leads to questioning of motives and actions. Non-communication creates the ideal conditions for a grapevine within the family where incorrect information may be passed around. Siblings and cousins compete for the position, pulling each other down. This negativity destroys the cohesiveness of a family, effectively damaging the business as well. When the time for succession comes, no one accepts the decision. On the contrary, clear communication helps others to build their lives around this decision. It gives time for the successor to be trained and be ready for the job. It helps the business plan for the long-term.

I) Have a robust advisory team

Let's face it. We all take advice before arriving at an important decision. Even if we don't reach out for advice to anyone consciously or subconsciously, our decisions are based on what we hear, see or read about a particular subject. So, isn't it advisable to hire the right talent to help you decide on the successor? Business families have chartered accountants and lawyers who are associated with the business and are invariably close to the family head. They have a tendency to give their own opinion on succession matters, and this advice can also be the kind that the head wants to hear; not necessarily the right one.

On the other hand, not taking any advice will always make you prone to choosing on the basis of a single perspective—your own. Hiring specialists helps you arrive at smarter solutions based on merit.

Depending on too many advisers also creates too many opinions. Business communities will speak from their own experiences, which differ from generation to generation, and may not be applicable to the generational situation you are in. Let's take my case: We are separating the ownership with management of business. We are in our third generation and loaded with numbers. My friend who is a first-generation owner himself, on hearing about our transformation, cautioned me that the children in the fourth generation won't have much to do with their time if they are out of the management of the business. This will make them go astray. He advised, 'Let them be in the day-to-day management.' This is how a first-generation businessperson will advise. There is nothing wrong in his advice if we were in the first generation, but with the growing numbers in the family, our objective is to ensure longevity of the business and financial stability of the family. Providing work for the family comes later, but it's the top priority for the first generation as business and family finances are secure. So, an experienced word of advice may, sometimes, not solve the objective that a certain generation is out to achieve.

In an environment where members are on a collision course, it is always a compromised candidate that gets chosen. He could be liked or, more importantly, not disliked by all. This cannot be the qualification to choose a successor. Such average choices will hamper business in the long run as they are mere consensus candidates than actual performers who can take the business to the next level.

J) Do not look for a clone

You are successful and have brought the company to where it is today. Your characteristics are currently in tune with the business and revenues are growing. It's just logical that someone like you will be the ideal candidate to be a successor. The 'just-like-me' person will suit the current situation but may need a different outlook to take the business to the future. We know, with time, old becomes obsolete as market dynamics, product segments and competitors change. Having a long-term business view while selecting a successor is more advisable than fulfilling a short-term requirement.

K) Target date of succession

Setting a date for succession points to identifying a timeline when all the stakeholders get time to sync in with the move. Transformation does take time. It cannot be a one-day event. Once the timeline is set, one has to introduce the plan to the organization for it to work. Creating a timeline is essential for identifying potential successors; and time is required to groom the chosen one to finally take charge. It also gives time to others to build their lives around this decision.

Succession is best used to transform a company. Some owners get cold feet when the actual date approaches, delaying the process. This questions their intent. The successor is already prepared; so is the organization. It will be difficult to hold him and chances of him overthrowing the board or leaving the business for greener pastures are strong.

During the development stage, I recommend that successors identify a mentor in a senior manager who has been loyal to the organization. Family businesses nurture such talent in abundance. This works in favour of the successor in building trust with the stakeholders.

As a conclusion to this sin of not having a succession plan, one should keep in mind that owners are the biggest assets of a family business. But they should not behave like fixed assets. Not creating a succession plan is a sin which has its impact on the business. It leaves the business headless in any eventuality.

Businesses must be kept disaster-proof and succession planning is its insurance policy.

Sin 28: Not Having a Family Office

Entrepreneurs start a business to meet the financial needs of self and family. We often hear amazing success stories of start-ups that came up first in garages, living rooms and shop floors. The first generation deploys all resources of the family into the business with the hope of deriving benefits in return. This expectation plants the seed of family dependence on the resources of the business. As business grows, so does the family. While business starts demanding more working members from the family, the latter may start utilizing company employees for personal work. Further, drawing salaries and enjoying perks like paid travel, telephone expenses, purchase of cars and their maintenance, and the education of children as it's considered returns on investment from the business point of view. The overlap of sets A and B is bound to increase when some families go to the extent of using employees for personal chores like booking holidays or travel tickets, fixing appointments and paying their bills. I have seen incidences where household expenses and even something as trivial as the expenses of keeping a pet at home are also paid for by the business.

When members increase, so does the personal workload. Families start to consume too much time of business employees, creating disturbances at work. There comes a breaking point when this gets addressed: by creating boundaries around what the business can take care of and what the household has to do for itself. The pre-defined list of tasks which the family can rely on the business for, is designated to a set of people, with whom the family interacts—this is the foundation of a family office.

Family offices do not have a standard role and I have noticed them having drastically different connotations from family to family. From routinely handling perks, tax, insurance and legal work, it can extend to whatever set A collectively decides for their working and non-working members. In cases where families own ancestral properties, estate maintenance and planning are included in the scope of the family office's work. Philanthropy is a major activity of business families and it is the business infrastructure that manages this. Families set up societies and trusts to be involved in charities like hospitals, operating schools, etc. Managing these trusts requires a competent set of people in the family office.

Larger families with multiple owners and successors sometimes create an outfit which is their judiciary system within the family. It plays a pivotal role in drafting the family rulebook that must impose multiple restrictions on the entry and exit of the successor. I have seen multiple family charters that have clear laid-down criteria for selecting the family member who will work on behalf of the family. The criteria start with academic qualifications, work experience in another industry for a certain number of years, or, more specifically, the experience of working in a competitor industry. Some families also give weightage to experience acquired in one's own business. What eventually comes out is an assortment of things that constitutes the family charter (as discussed earlier) which is guarded by this family office. The family office, in such cases, is not just responsible for managing and upgrading the charter but also for taking decisions in case of conflicts.

Structure of a Family Office

Now the question that arises is—who should be a part of such a conflict-resolving family office? It all depends on how many members you want to keep in your family office and what kind of conflicts you see arising. But, at the same time, it is important to make sure that all the owners are represented righteously in the family office. These are the following people whom you can consider for a family office:

a) Elders of the family who have worked with the business (father, uncle, grandfather, etc.)
b) Non-working elders who are owners (for example, a wise aunt)
c) Non-working members who may not have ownership but a friendly stake (for example, wives)
d) If required, a lawyer, a CA or CS who has been associated with the family for a long time

The family office, which is usually set up to resolve conflicts, eventually becomes an investing office. The family office decides what is to be done with the money which resides within the business and is available to be invested for the profit of the family, since the owners managing the management only control the profitability of the business and not the wealth of the family. Investment and wealth management become essential for a successful family business. The availability of specialized investment firms has prompted families to outsource this activity, but some prefer to operate two family offices—one to meet personal lifestyle needs of members and the other for wealth management. In fact, we also see families having multiple family offices dedicated to different needs.

Families can have single or multiple family offices; the objective is to manage the needs of set A—the family. If one commits this sin of not having a family office, they will have uninformed and dissatisfied family members scrambling to be part of the management to derive benefits for personal gain. A family office also helps the family exit from the management when the time is right.

Sin 29: Not Having an Exit Policy

While it is important to have a succession plan, it is just as important to have an exit policy. It is usually assumed that an exit policy is for the whole family to exit the business by selling it. That would be termed as an ownership monetization plan.

The other exit is from the management by selecting a CFR, a person who is jointly selected by the family to represent it in the business. This form of exit cannot be classified as an exit as it's part of succession-planning. Then what exit are we talking about? It is critical to note that there has to be an exit policy for the individual equity owner of the family business.

In India, like divorce, exiting a family is considered taboo. Most families are not prepared to face both eventualities. They make amends in situations and adjust relationships based on the motto: till death do us part. For instance, older generations have strong views on divorce. The bride must arrive in a wedding palanquin and only leave in a coffin. Similarly for the male member; he is born here and will die here.

Such strong social customs are reasons why family businesses don't have very efficient exit policies. They are, in fact, apprehensive of addressing the issue of the exit of members. It is viewed as a value judgement on the family business. There is a ring of suspicion and a feeling of being short-changed.

On the business side, if a key family member leaves, it can have an impact, with employees too leaving and the dilution of commitment towards the business by other stakeholders like suppliers and dealers. In a public limited company, the loss of wealth is a possibility.

When anyone decides to exit their family, there are mixed reactions from the common people and the extended family. Imagine when it happens in your own immediate family—the first reaction is that of getting everyone to stay together due to a herd mentality and efforts are made to keep it that way. Slowly, members start reacting differently with varying emotions like hurt, disappointment and anger. This is a selfish outburst; the family is only seeing it from their perspective. It has to be viewed with empathy as to why a member wants to sever ties. It should not be all about 'me' but about them too. Therefore, an exit policy has to be created and it should be devoid of emotions as different members may want to exit for different reasons.

An individual may exit because he has a fantastic opportunity to start something and needs capital which can come only by selling one's own holding. On the other hand, there are members whose own personal vision is not in tune with the existing family business and they don't see their future with the business. Their DNA is different. There are also family verticals that start something new, become big and don't want to associate with the existing brand, business or the family, and hence, demand a fair exit.

Sometimes, warring sides in the family stage an exit drama to take control of the business. Having an exit policy diminishes such possibilities. On the other hand, family verticals that have no power or say in the business feel disconnected and eventually sell their stake to outsiders to even out with the family. An exit policy safeguards and covers all such eventualities.

Creating a family council with the sole purpose of keeping the family connected and satisfied is recommended, especially where the exit of members may upset the shareholding matrix. Since it's a priority of the family, it is often made a part of the family office. The council routinely organizes get-togethers and interactions among family members, besides business interactions, with the sole purpose of bonding. This helps maintain a healthy environment. Communication and trust increase and strengthen the bond among family members; it builds a stronger identity for the family, satisfying each member's recognition needs. It also makes dispute resolution easier.

Families, at times, can get complicated and working with family members may not be everyone's cup of tea, nor cohabiting in a not-so-flexible joint family set-up. Some verticals are uneasy with the number of members and the power politics that come with shareholding percentages. It can get daunting to deal with all this. Somewhere down the line, everyone looks for an opportunity to exit, especially if a member is feeling trapped. You can't tie a person down because limiting their scope and opportunities will result in frustration, which would hamper the business in the long run. It is impossible to hold on to someone who feels trapped. Therefore, for its survival, the family business has to be robust with an exit policy for everyone, be it an individual member, a vertical of the family, its CFR, or the successor.

While we are on the topic of the CFR as well as the successor, what needs to be understood with regard to the exit policy is that while the successor gets appropriate market value for his holding, for the family–owner–CFR, two levels of exit policy are recommended. First, in the context of management, and second, in the context of ownership.

Betrayal is a big reason why members or even the entire vertical of the family demand an exit. Betrayal is an outcome of over-ambition. Choosing ambition over family destroys trust. The act of betrayal, indulged in knowingly, or as a result of oversight, makes the person who has been deceived, bitter. They strongly feel that it could have been prevented. The desire for an exit is fair as they do not want to be recipients of further high-handedness, greed, deceit and power play. Once bitten, twice shy, they say!

Let's look at the brighter side: exit policies give the family business an opportunity to have a leaner ownership pattern, thus ensuring further continuity for generations. Having said that, I have some advice for members who decide to exit: Don't burn your bridges; you still carry the family name with you and the advantages that accompany it. Keep a window open for any probability of a re-entry. The future is uncertain; there are times when exiting members seek re-entry and, at times, the family offers an opportunity to a member who has exited, to re-join. Remember, a family business is like Hotel California, you can check out any time you like but you can never leave.

An exit, to be considered right, must be for an opportunity and not to escape tensions already brewing in the family environment. The most recommended way to exit is to be transparent about the reasons for departure since there might be speculation regarding the exit.

In the battle of Kurukshetra, the Kaurava army create a *chakravyuh*, an impregnable battle formation, which only the creator, Dronacharya, and his favourite disciple, Arjun, knew how to break out of and emerge victorious. By a twist of fate, Abhimanyu had learnt how to break into one from his father, Arjun. He did so successfully when confronted with the formation in battle, but, alas, he did not know the way out—the exit. Family businesses cannot become a chakravyuh that one cannot get out of. Death was certain for Abhimanyu as he did not possess the knowledge to exit. On learning about the death of his sixteen-year-old warrior son, the vengeful father, Arjun, along with his brothers, went on a rampage, slaughtering and eliminating the Kaurava dynasty, resulting in the demolition of the Kauravas and their empire.

Trapping dissatisfied souls within the family is a sin of destruction one must totally avoid. The freedom to exit must form a part of a charter and is a torch of liberty.

Sanyas T4:
Figure 12

FOURTH STAGE

STAGE	ASHRAM	4 Ts	GOAL
I 	Brahmacharya	Training	Knowledge
II 	Grihastha	Transaction	Wealth
III 	Vanaprastha	Transition	Fame
IV 	Sanyas	Turn-in	Relinquishment

Sanyas means complete renunciation. It comes from the Sanskrit word 'Sam-nyas'. Sam means total, Nyas means abandonment. So complete abandonment is what Sanyas is. The definition of the word in Sanskrit elaborates that the perfect abandonment of one's material, emotional and intellectual self is the true intent of Sanyas. In a business context, it is rather the abandonment of operations (material), of guidance and governance (intellectual) and ownership (emotional) that will help one attain Sanyas.

Vanaprastha focuses on detachment and handing over of management, a phase of semi-retirement. The journey undertaken at this stage of transition culminates in destination Sanyas, the stage of renunciation. The final of the four ashrams, where one takes complete retirement from business by handing over ownership. The two questions that commonly arise at this stage or while preparing for this stage are, how do I do it, or why should I completely exit? Let's understand the how and the why of it.

In Brahmacharya, a child's physical and mental faculties are growing and developing every day. In Sanyas, the reverse starts to happen. The process of ageing enters the geriatric phase in which, first and foremost, one experiences sensory changes, followed by organ malfunctions. Physically too, body mass and the nervous system start to degenerate and managing hereditary ailments becomes more challenging. Self-care becomes a priority and rightly so! When the focus shifts to looking after oneself, it leaves little or no room for any other work. In the interest of the business, the next generation and self, it is advisable to denounce business and stay focused on the self.

The act of relinquishment may be unique to each owner, and their actions can broadly be classified and attributed as:

i) Organized
ii) Self-centred
iii) Disorganized

On a lighter note, I would call them the good, the bad and the ugly of relinquishment. The good way is when the handover is planned and executed in a structured way, giving the three stakeholders (the business, the generation receiving and the generation handing over) clarity and security to blossom. Business requires progressive promoters and an able leader; the next generation looks for clarity of ownership and the relinquishing owner has to secure himself financially for the rest of his life. This is an ideal method and it is called a systematic and organized exit.

There are owners who think only about themselves and stay secretive regarding their next moves. This could be as drastic as selling the business or their stake to an outsider for personal monetary gains. This move is unfavourable and perceived as bad as it only takes into account the individual need of one stakeholder. The other two stakeholders, the business and the next generation, need to be part of the decision-making process as the three sets overlap each other. This is termed as a selfish exit.

The act of relinquishing becomes ugly when the owner abandons the business. Abandonment due to fatigue, terminal illness, death or indecision leaves behind chaos and conflicts. The owner is responsible for the business and the next generation. Leaving something midway without finishing the final handover of ownership is a disorganized exit. This could be due to unavoidable emergencies or, simply, indecision. It causes irreparable damage to the family business. The turn-in stage encourages and allows the owner to exit with eyes wide open.

If there is life after death, there is definitely life after total retirement. The handing over of management during Vanaprastha is indeed a process of learning to detach, and, hence, the final renunciation of ownership of business becomes easy in Sanyas. Till now, one has been working for money; now is the time when money has to work for you! You have just exited the drama company you owned and have also been replaced by a younger lead in the play.

You can sit in the audience and watch the play with the new lead performing and the new owner executing the business, or move out of the theatre and explore the outside world. The choice is entirely yours. You may want to delink or keep stalking the business. You are not old, so don't behave like you are—you have a full stage ahead of you, so live your Sanyas. You have to live your life and forget your age. C.S. Lewis had said, 'You are never too old to set another goal or to dream another dream.' It means you can get out of the business you have been operating and can renounce it all to begin something that you have always wanted to do. That's the only way to take the person out of business.

Geriatric studies bifurcate this stage into three sections from the point of view of managing oneself: young–old, old and old–old. Personally speaking, I believe that though age is visible on the skin, it actually resides in the mind. This is the reason why the duration of sub-stages is very personal. Most continue the philanthropy started in Vanaprastha in the first sub-stage of young–old and some embark on the path of self-fulfilment. The ones in old–old are mostly at a divine sub-stage.

In Maslow's hierarchy of needs, self-actualization is at the top of the pyramid. What is self-actualization? When one feels satisfied at having achieved one's potential, it is known as true self-actualization. It should not be linked to success and status which one has already acquired in Grihastha and Vanaprastha. It's more holistic, encompassing ones psychological needs. A 'bucket list' is also a rudimentary example of attaining self-actualization. The creative side of every person has desires that need to be fulfilled; the first two sub-stages of Sanyas help one reach the final pinnacle of self-actualization and complete the need to attain self-satisfaction.

Following a passion is a common phenomenon. A friend of mine, a cardio surgeon, started walnut farming in the US.

There are several others out there who start new ventures as a life-after-family-business backup—a true entrepreneurial mindset. My father-in-law, on the other hand, took a sabbatical; time off to relax and revisit his family heritage of Ramayana and Krishnayan, two epics written by his own grandfather. He also directed his earnings towards the renovation and reconstruction of dilapidated community structures such as parks, temples, shelters, etc. Truly a value-based decision! He tells me, 'After denouncing business, work for a cause and not applause; seek happiness and shun selfishness as life in this stage has to be expressed and not impressed.'

Detachment should not be perceived as a negative emotion. It is not a state of being estranged or having a lack of empathy. Turn-in, in fact, is positive—a state of calmness. The skill of shedding of desires avoids stress and maintains the mind and body balance. Detachment provides inner calm, an attitude of open-mindedness and a practical approach. Remember, you are in Sanyas and you have to ultimately become a sanyasi. As per Vedic teachings, a sanyasi should be a friend of the self, with no self-destruction or inner conflict, free from desires, a contented soul, even-minded, with no prejudices, a self-conqueror, with balance and restraint of mind and soul, for staying undisturbed and attaining liberation from suffering.

This stage helps you explore and awaken the creative potential that has been lying dormant. And if you do not forgo the business, you will not be able to awaken it or let go of the business. Only something that is extremely interesting and creative will help you get detached from business which has been your life for decades. It also works in reverse— if you don't let the business go, you will never be able to explore the plethora of options awaiting you. But this is my own thinking and aspiration of my own Sanyas.

But what's natural in Sanyas is the ease of giving, not from a feeling of guilt or out of gratitude, but a sense of happiness. I have watched my father and many family elders get immense satisfaction in sharing or parting with what they had accumulated. Most have wealth or time. My father also had knowledge, experience and imagination. He wanted people around him to be successful and happy. He would invite his friends and acquaintances, and, while it would look like he was inviting them socially, he was actually listening to their problems and helping them by offering all the wisdom that he had acquired in his lifetime.

He would support them monetarily and use his influence and network to help them build a future for themselves and uplift them from their current stature. He enjoyed finding solutions where there seemed to be none. For him, it was like playing a game or solving a puzzle. It gave him immense happiness and a feeling of self-worth. They say creativity is intelligence having fun and, in my father's case, it was so. That was his own self-actualization and his own creative way of indulging. It is important to enjoy your wealth in Vanaprastha and create a purpose for living, but, more importantly, to use this wealth towards achieving it in Sanyas.

So, the definition of creative is also not limited to what would be defined as conventionally creative. Sanyas is the stage which is truly yours. You have earned it after working all your life and it is up to you to make sure that you make the best use of this stage.

The process of detachment is gratifying and takes one to another level of wisdom. It's a positive state of well-being and happiness. Once you embrace Sanyas, you stop clinging to things. By the time one reaches old–old, truth has dawned upon them and one is more accepting towards the eventuality of life's biggest truth, of life coming to an end. Unfortunately, all cannot achieve this bliss; there are some who are constantly questioning themselves.

How can I leave? I have no financial security. What will I do if I quit business? These are questions in Sanyas from a person who did not follow his Vanaprastha.

Owners cannot hand the business over because primarily, their own identity is so intermixed with the business, that they cannot see themselves without it. For some, the routine and relationships cannot be given up in one day and the thought of a sudden exit can be very disturbing. If transition was not followed during Vanaprastha, to let go at this age and stage becomes impossible. Holding on with no plan but fear brings us to the final sin of life.

Sin 30: Not Relinquishing Ownership

Possessions stay back on this planet, only ownership changes. All the material things that we gather, do not go with us to the other world; the pharaohs tried to take it along with them when they were buried in the pyramids, only to be looted by thieves or taken away by museums. If we cannot carry our wealth to our graves, then let me ask you some introspective questions. What will happen to your possessions after your death? Isn't it advisable to donate, gift or allocate it to someone? Whether your wealth will depreciate, be looted or taken away, will depend on the way you detach yourself from it.

Relinquishment of ownership is mandatory as it ensures financial security. This statement may sound shocking, but it's true, because it pushes one to plan for continuity of the business and, on the flip side, ensures one's own financial stability and security. Own covers self, spouse, incapacitated family members and those who are dependent on you. When one has to exit the business totally, one is compelled to plan out a future for themselves. Stability comes from a regular income and investments, while security is guaranteed through insurance and savings.

The most basic financial need starts with maintaining living standards. Covering medical expenses takes the second spot. Next, financial stability is required to pursue philanthropy and for achieving self-actualization. Having the freedom to spend on whatever one wants is the ultimate luxury one can achieve by efficient planning. Two pointers to be kept in mind during financial planning are: to be debt-free and to have an insurance plan in place. What most people forget to factor into the plan which is highly recommended is an emergency fund. The future holds unforeseen expenses, and, at times, one may live longer than expected. Whatever one's life, the core idea is to plan and live with peace of mind.

Once secure, ownership can be handed over in any form. Some do it through forming a trust, while others simply transfer or gift it. If it forms a part of the plan, it can be allocated through a will. While signing of papers is the easier part, what is difficult is breaking the strongest bond that exists between the owner and the business.

When detachment is both ways, it is achievable. But if the business or the owner develops the insecurity of being the rejected party, they become stalkers. The business can feel that they don't have the right leadership and hence, keep coming back to the former owner for solutions. The senior management, at times, keeps pursuing the owner and doesn't let them break away. It's common to see clients chase the owner as they have been dealing with them. Such stalking of owners by the business is common, but can be settled over a short period of time.

On the other hand, if the owner cannot bear this separation, it becomes worse. Businesses often cannot deal with such a situation as it can get distracting, frustrating and stressful to avoid the interference of the ex-owner. It also carries a functional risk to the new team and the business.

Stalking by the owner can be through physically appearing on the premises or sending queries and suggestions through mail. Giving gifts or befriending management is also a form of staying in touch and not detaching. This obsession about the old partner is only when one is lonely and has not found a purpose in later life. At times, they are still attached to the name and fame of the business; the insecurity of losing something that was their own identity keeps bringing them back to the business. In some cases, they feel cheated after leaving: when the business needed them, they were there; now, when they need the business, the business is no longer paying them any attention. This fear of being left alone when the need is stronger is depressing and makes one stalk the business.

It's a virtue to be loyal and committed and my father took pride in it. The strong character that he was, he was devoted to the business and felt responsible towards it. Owners with such high value systems feel obligated towards the business due to a sense of duty, as they would towards their life partner—commitment until death. It was only when he was physically weak and could see sibling conflicts, that he let go completely. For some, it becomes a matter of heart over head as they love their work and it is always difficult to leave your love.

People with stronger emotions make detaching more painful for themselves. Letting go means letting go of the past. Something which successful entrepreneurs are proud of. It gives them self-worth in old age. And it is this past which gives them the impetus to live. Renunciation, in our context, means complete detachment from the business. However, it doesn't mean complete detachment from the family or the name that has been created so far. A sanyasi surrenders his home and possessions (in this case the business) because he perceives the whole universe as his home.

Business stalwarts, due to their popularity with the media, fulfil their need to stay attached to fame by representing the brand and indulging in public relations. In this role that is defined for them, they represent the business and the family at various platforms as a brand ambassador. It's a platonic relationship which is helpful to both. One can devote time to the media from a position of authority and respect due to one's status, commenting not just on business but also on current affairs, based on past experiences and achievements. The essence remains the same—that you renounce the business while being an asset from the outside. If you stay in business, you actually become a liability to it and the family. It may sound shockingly rude, but it is the bitter truth that with age, humans become emotionally weak, which influences informed decision-making, thus harming the business and family in the long run.

Relinquishing or allocating ownership creates new owners. Though they may have been trained and skilled for the role, there is always a final critical password which needs to be shared, which completes the handing over of ownership. Most businesses have a USP and this key knowledge is retained with the owners. It could be a flavour of the product, or its fragrance. It could be a formulation, or process knowledge. Some businesses have trade secrets and some have financial or client control. This knowledge must get successfully inherited by the new owner.

In the early 1960s, the Baidyanath family was faced with the sudden demise of my grandfather, leaving the family without a clear leadership. I dread to even visualize the power struggle and chaos that must have occurred at the time. Fortunately, the family and business survived. All businesses may not have had the same luck. In family businesses, emotions of non-working members play a critical role in succession planning. More so in the event of there being none. My grandmother, I believe, played a role in this survival. While the family and I are immensely thankful and grateful to our grand old lady, all families may not be fortunate to have such blessings.

Business owners must acknowledge the importance of ownership (set C) and not stay in the realm of family (set A) and business (set B) to complete the essence of Sanyas, that is turn-in. Time to call it a day! Retire and save the family business from being affected by this sin!

4 Ts: TRAIN, TRANSACT, TRANSITION, TURN-IN

STAGE		ASHRAM	4 Ts	GOAL
I		Brahmacharya	Training	Knowledge
II		Grihastha	Transaction	Wealth
III		Vanaprastha	Transition	Fame
IV		Sanyas	Turn-in	Relinquishment

STAGE		ASHRAM	4 Ts	GOAL
I		Brahmacharya	Training	Knowledge
II		Grihastha	Transaction	Wealth
III		Vanaprastha	Transition	Fame
IV		Sanyas	Turn-in	Relinquishment

STAGE		ASHRAM	4 Ts	GOAL
I		Brahmacharya	Training	Knowledge
II		Grihastha	Transaction	Wealth
III		Vanaprastha	Transition	Fame
IV		Sanyas	Turn-in	Relinquishment

STAGE		ASHRAM	4 Ts	GOAL
I		Brahmacharya	Training	Knowledge
II		Grihastha	Transaction	Wealth
III		Vanaprastha	Transition	Fame
IV		Sanyas	Turn-in	Relinquishment

Often, I am part of conversations where the topic gravitates towards life, families and family businesses. I have noticed a pattern in these discussions. People normally have very generic views on life, like life is what you make of it; or life is to be lived. The majority who speak from experience have opinions that are more specific; for example, life is hard work, or what is life without family. The successful ones will be humble with their point of views—life is a blessing, or life is all luck. Life for some is fun while there are others for whom life is hell. The most profound opinion being that life is a transaction. Why?

While the Swiss economy is known for precision, Japan was built on hard work after the devastation caused by World War II. Globally, the opinion that prevails is that India is a land of relationships and America, without doubt, was built on transactions. The largest economy has its impact on economic organizations like family businesses. Hence, the primary importance is given to transactions.

When conversations become more magnanimous, people start emphasizing two attributes of life: life is 80 per cent hard work and 20 per cent luck, or statements like: life is opportunities and relationships. There is a distinct shift from life being addressed as one particular thing to two or three. One can hear comments like life is knowledge and transactions, or the more famous one being, life is desire, knowledge and action. In all the conversations, life for most will remain within the boundaries of Brahmacharya and Grihastha. People need to look beyond and acknowledge the full life span. Life is a circle which we all must complete. Family business must gravitate towards my theory of the four Ts and live it.

There is a mention in the Bible of the three wise men from the east. It's time to relook at wisdom from the east, the knowledge of our ancient scriptures and my experiences clearly define life as four Ts—train, transact, transition and turn-in. These four Ts of the generational cycle are a road map for all to follow. It is holistic and sustainable generation after generation in family business. I look forward to generations living as per the recommended four stages. One day, I hope to hear in conversations, that life is four Ts. That is the day I will know that my book has made a difference and had an impact on family business, making my own Vanaprastha successful.

A shloka from thousands of years ago explains the essence of the four stages of life beautifully, giving importance to the need to acquire knowledge to gain wealth, and then fame to ultimately help one renounce it all and embrace Sanyas.

प्रथमेनार्जिता विद्या द्वितीयेनार्जितं धनं ।
तृतीयेनार्जितः कीर्तिः चतुर्थे किं करिष्यति ॥

अर्थ: जिसने प्रथम अर्थात ब्रह्मचर्य आश्रम में विद्या अर्जित नहीं की, द्वितीय अर्थात गृहस्थ आश्रम में धन अर्जित नहीं किया, तृतीय अर्थात वानप्रस्थ आश्रम में कीर्ति अर्जित नहीं की, वह चतुर्थ अर्थात संन्यास आश्रम में क्या करेगा?

Meaning, if you have not acquired knowledge during Brahmacharya; have not acquired wealth in Grihastha; haven't received fame in Vanaprastha, then what are you going to do (renounce) in the fourth—the Sanyas ashram?

In the context of this book, an individual must respect and pass through these four stages of life for crisis avoidance. This lifecycle must be planned and followed diligently, stage by stage. If you have acquired knowledge and wealth in Brahmacharya and Grihastha respectively, but not transitioned into Vanaprastha to experience recognition and fame, you may not be able to complete your lifecycle by reaching Sanyas. One who achieves one's share of knowledge, wealth and fame is a satisfied soul, who can easily relinquish them for Sanyas. If the achievements are not complete, how do you relinquish? One will keep trying to acquire them, with little or no success, thus disturbing the balance of the journey of a family business through generations. Similarly, if you have acquired knowledge and not wealth, your quest for the acquisition of wealth will continue, delaying your transition (Vanaprastha) and ultimately the turn-in (Sanyas), thus hampering the generational cycle and the continuity of business.

It Is a Complete Circle

In Brahmacharya, you are part of a family. You focus on education. You have no role to play in business. When you enter Grihastha, you get married, raise a family, get into the business and become part of the family business. In Vanaprastha, you start distancing yourself from the business as you have already done your bit by contributing immensely in terms of value and wealth creation for the family business. And in the Sanyas stage, you retire. You detach yourself from the business and are back to being a member of the family.

Brahma, Vishnu and Mahesh

Brahma, Vishnu and Mahesh have distinctive roles and represent the inter-generational characteristics displayed by each generation. However, one's behaviour and attitude are also formed due to early influences like the year of birth, the pressures of formative years or events surrounding the impressionable age. Reason enough for any one of these behaviours to be seen in a member of either generation. For our understanding, we can map these characteristics, of any family member belonging to any generation, to see their personality type—the outcome will reveal how they will act or react to situations.

The personality types are classified into three.
Brahma type—aggressive
Vishnu type—passive
Mahesh type—assertive

Each type will display the following responses:

The Brahma type will stay optimistic, strong, and dictatorial. They will treat the business as their offspring as they either started it or grew it exponentially. They will project themselves to be bigger than the business.

The Vishnu type will stay rational, calm, composed. They will take the business along with care and responsibility—like an elder sibling or as one would take care of an ageing parent.

The Mahesh type will stay unpredictable, temperamental, prone to extreme reactions, and will treat the business as inherited wealth.

Saam, Daam, Dand, Bhed: Understanding an Ancient Law of Management

Chanakya, who lived in the third century BCE, was a philosopher and a royal adviser who devised laws and theories to ensure smooth governance. His Chanakya Neeti is famous and followed even today, in the twenty-first century. My core principle of management is derived from Chanakya's wisdom related to the actions: *Saam, Daam, Dand* and *Bhed*. I have applied this, time and again, in my business and seen positive results.

All situations can be solved by any of these four methods. Saam—things can be achieved by logical and convincing explanations. Daam—there is a price for everything and it must be paid to get required results. Dand—imposing curbs and restrictions by applying physical pressure or causing suffering. Bhed—creating differences, dividing the group, or exposing secrets, are the distinct characteristics of this method. My personal advice, which I have gained from my experiences, is to remember the sequence, and never jump the gun.

Good management practices and the essence of this theory are following the sequence of implementation.

To stop a sin from being committed, the first step is Saam—dialogue. Explain and highlight the disadvantages of committing that sin. Make yourself, the individual or the group, arrive at a shared meaning and understanding. It is not a debate of what is right or wrong, but a dialogue to arrive at a solution.

If that doesn't work, you resort to Daam—compensation. It is not a bribe; it is a compensation for services provided in the form of a reward or an incentive. Receiving benefits like monetary compensation or a position translates into a win-win situation. Most issues get resolved between Saam and Daam.

If Daam fails, you resort to Dand—punishment. The fear of being penalized makes a person think again before committing a sin. If one does not act right, they must suffer the consequences. Suffering emotional, mental or physical pain is a deterrent. The certainty of a strict penalty can bring the situation under control and discourage a person from committing a sin.

If Dand is ineffective, and the situation is very complex and seems to be getting out of hand, you come to the last and the most lethal way, Bhed—create differences or alienate. An end-of-the-road, no-way-out situation, threatening to reveal a secret achieves the desired result. Stripping a person of authority, support or power renders them irrelevant and stops them from committing a sin.

How to Thrive in a Family Business is Saam—sharing wisdom which is applicable in both, prosperous and challenging journeys of a family business. The core purpose being continuity, for which survival and growth of the business are essential. Practising the 4 Ts of a lifecycle provides change for growth.

ACKNOWLEDGEMENTS

This book would not have been possible without Meesha, my wife. Her encouragement and support throughout the journey of life and, specifically while writing this book, has been immense.

To each and every member of the Baidyanath family who, knowingly or unknowingly, gave me the experiences and made me who I am today, thank you!

Gratitude to my uncle, Ram Krishan Sharma, for being a teacher, guide, and a pillar of support.

No acknowledgement would be complete without mentioning Krishna Aunty and her husband, Lt Colonel (Retd) S.P. Sharma.

Special thanks to Professor V.K. Murthy of SP Jain Institute of Management and Research; and my dear friend, Vivek Kohli.

I would also like to thank those who shared a part of their life's experiences with me and gave their inputs to make specific sins more relatable.

In alphabetical order:

B.K. Goswami
Gaurav Gupta
Madhav Shriram
Pratima Kirloskar
Saeed Shervani
Shishir Nevatia
Siddharth Prasad

Last, but not least, my children! Kudos to my son, Rishi Raj, for his silent and stoic support in bearing with me—a special thank you for suggesting the working title *Sons and Sins;* and daughter, Veerangana, for her immense contribution towards critically evaluating the manuscript and pointing out its flaws in a positive way. She gave inputs that helped me to see the book in a new light and forced me to work on its shortcomings. What you have today is a result of our joint hard work.

NOTE FROM THE AUTHOR

Advantage—Family Business

To take advantage, we need to first identify if a family business actually exists. So, what qualifies as a family business?

A business started by a father/parent is only a business till their offspring does not join it. If even one child joins the business, it qualifies as a family business. Similarly, if two siblings start a business, it is only a partnership. It becomes a family business only when the children join in. A business should have multi-generations owning and operating it, for it to qualify as a family business.

A healthy business with a potential for growth in the long run, a cohesive family unit, and a proud legacy are ideal for nearly every family business. Today, the young generation is proud of this legacy and sees it as an opportunity. But it was not so until the recent past. Children joining the family business were looked down upon. People doubted their capabilities and entrepreneurship skills. It was seen as an easy way out to earn money. Successors started avoiding family businesses and chose different career paths, not out of passion, but just to prove a point, harming the future prospects of the family business.

Things are different today! Their existence cannot be ignored. They are the biggest contributors to the economies of their respective countries (barring communist countries), which, in turn, support other forms of ownership businesses to prosper. Successors are intelligently skilling themselves to continue the legacy. It is no longer a succession of necessity; rather, it is seen as an opportunity succession. Family businesses are now confidently hiring non-family executives to focus on growth strategies. Professionals, who are eager to contribute their skills towards the growth of the country's economy, are now attracted towards these organizations, increasing the available pool of talent. A good CXO team is attracted towards a family business when they see opportunities, compensation and independence of operation.

My advice for all family business members is to get out of your comfort zone, keep aside the 'I', dream a future, ignore the critics and sprint into creating a legacy out of your business.

Extension of the copyright page

Disclaimer

The views and opinions expressed in this book are solely based on the author's own knowledge and understanding of business strategies and do not reflect the views and/or opinions of any other person. The examples used in the book are for illustrative purposes only and have been compiled from research findings, resources and references available in the public domain, and from sources for which the requisite permissions are available with the author. The author has made every effort to ensure the information within this book is correct at the time of publication; however, there are no representations or warranties, express or implied, about the accuracy, reliability or suitability of the same. The book is strictly for educational purposes. If you wish to apply ideas contained in this book, you are taking full responsibility for your actions. The author does not assume and hereby disclaims any liability to any party for any loss, damage, or disruption caused by errors or omissions, whether such errors or omissions result from accident, negligence, or any other cause and the author and the publishers are not in any way liable for the same.